What

is

Remembered

by

Alice

B.

Toklas

North Point Press · *San Francisco* · *1985*

Library of Congress Catalogue Card Number: 84–62304
ISBN: 0–86547–180–0

What
is
Remembered

1

I WAS born and raised in California, where my maternal grandfather had been a pioneer before the state was admitted to the Union. He had bought a gold mine and settled in Jackson, Amador County. A few years later he crossed the Isthmus of Panama again and went to Brooklyn, where he married my grandmother. There my mother was born. When she was three years old, they went to Jackson.

When they arrived in San Francisco all the bells were ringing. My grandmother said it was not a holiday, what were they celebrating? Two horse thieves are being hanged on Lone Mountain, was the response. It was an unpleasant welcome and my grandmother never forgot it.

As my grandfather's mine was not worth working, he sold it and bought a large tract of land in the San Joaquin Valley and turned to ranching. Later his stepsister's husband acquired a piece of land near his. It was they who organized the opposition to the Southern Pacific railroad and the defense against its laying tracks to carry the San Joaquin Valley harvest east. They were violently opposed to its having a monopoly, and they placed a barrage of farm implements across the road. The engine was forced to stop before it. The next day, however, it drove into the barricade and the railroad men laid tracks beyond. This constituted a right of way. Frank Norris took this as the theme for *The Octopus*, the first novel of his trilogy on the history of wheat.

There were no suitable schools in Amador County for my mother and her sister, nor music for my grandmother. So my grandfather moved his family to San Francisco, and while he built a home for them they lived at the Nucleus Hotel. The home he built on O'Farrell Street was where they lived for many years. The two girls grew up there and were married from there, I was born there, and later the two grandparents died there.

My mother with a group of ladies brought Emma Marwedel, a pupil of Froebel, to San Francisco, where in a large garden a schoolhouse had been built and the first kindergarten in the United States established. There I went mornings and learned to read and to write German and English, a great deal of geography, and some arithmetic.

It was when I was seven or eight that my grandmother

talked to me about music and took me to hear it. The first singer I remember was Judic, a gay though very old Parisian light opera singer. She wore an immense turquoise brooch surrounded by diamonds presented to her by the Emperor Louis Napoleon. That was my first introduction to the War of 1870.

There was then and for many years after a stock company, the Tivoli Opera House, that gave opera the year round, performing everything from *Aïda* to *Les Cloches de Corneville*. I enjoyed them all equally. It was there that I heard *Lohengrin* for the first time. Luisa Tetrazzini sang Violetta at the Tivoli, her cadenzas being so sensational that she was engaged for the Metropolitan Opera of New York.

My grandmother started to give me piano lessons and told me that she and her three sisters had been pupils of Friedrich Wieck, the father of Clara Schumann. When one of the sisters became a concert pianist in Vienna her parents disinherited her. Then she married an army officer, which was the last we heard of Tante Berthe.

When I was nine years old my father took me to spend the night with my grandparents. This was always a pleasure for me. The next morning my father called for me saying, I have a surprise for you, there is a baby brother for you to see. Is it Tommie? I asked.

Tommie was a small marble Renaissance head my mother had, for which I had a passionate attachment. No, I don't think so, my father answered. You will see.

When I did see the small red-faced thing, I was ready to burst into tears. I wanted to kiss my mother and confide my horror to her. He is red like a lobster, I said, are you going to love him? Taking me in her arms she said, Not like you, darling, you will always come first. And I was satisfied.

It was at this time that my parents decided to go to Europe to celebrate the golden wedding anniversary of my father's parents.

My mother and I found New York very cold. On a chair with runners a cousin pushed me on the frozen lake in Central Park, whilst my father and cousins skated, making figures on the ice.

To get to the steamer we were obliged to be ferried to Hoboken. The boat got stuck and it was necessary to cut away the ice. But on the steamer on the Atlantic the sun shone, and for the twelve days of the voyage I played on deck.

At Hamburg where the steamer landed we went to see the Rentz circus, where not only trained horses but elephants danced to the music of a big blaring brass band.

From Hamburg we went to Kempen in Silesia, where my father's numerous family welcomed us and we were joined by the cousins and an uncle and an aunt from New York and two uncles from New Mexico.

My father's father was a gentle kindly person. He read aloud to me Grimm's fairy tales, frightening by comparison with those of Hans Christian Andersen and those of Perrault which I had already known. As a young man he had gone from home on a voyage to Portugal and in '48 he had clandestinely left his wife to go to Paris to fight on the barricades. My grandmother, not sympathizing with this escapade, had notified the bank in Paris not to honor her husband's cheques, thus obliging him to return to Kempen.

My grandfather enjoyed painting and gave one of the pictures he had painted to my father. It was a lively scene of two Polish cavalrymen with several wounded and dead Russian soldiers on the ground. The Poles were slashing at the two remaining Russians with broad swords.

My grandmother was a large, handsome, imperious woman who wore very long diamond earrings. In her white hair, piled very high, were artificial lilacs. She and my grandfather lived to be over eighty years old and died within a day of each other.

From Kempen my father drove us in a four-in-hand to Stettin to see a companion of his lycée days. It was at Stettin, at a restaurant, that some Polish officers asked my mother's permission to give me a glass of champagne so that everyone might toast the United States.

From Kempen we went to Vienna, and from there to Pest where my parents had some friends. In the music room the young people were dancing with Hungarian officers. For them I danced the cachucha and waltzed with the daughters of our host, Stephanie and Melanie, becoming quite dizzy as they did not reverse.

From Pest we went by way of Vienna and Dresden to England. My mother had found in Kempen a young Polish governess for me who was a pleasant companion, but as she spoke English perfectly I didn't learn any more Polish than my father had already taught me, "The Lord's Prayer" and "God Save Poland," which I forgot over a half-century ago.

In England we went to stay with my mother's uncle, who had married a Scotchwoman. They had two little daughters, Violet and Adela, about my age, and lived in the country. After a few days my parents decided to leave me there and go to London. The two cousins were sweet companions. But one night Violet woke me and said, Come quickly, Adela is walking in her sleep on a balcony without a railing. Adela had her eyes open but evidently was not seeing where she was nor where she was going. It was frightening but romantic.

Not as frightening, but quite as romantic, was the elephants' tusk jelly served to us children by an Indian colonel for tea when we were driven over to visit him.

From England we went back to Hamburg to stay with my mother's other uncle, a doctor who lived with his wife and widowed daughter and two very large black poodles that sat on their haunches immovable while we were being served my first frozen puddings. I remember a Nesselrode and a Himalaya. The poodles were each then given a large tray of coffee with milk. When they had finished this, the valet removed these trays and replaced them with two other trays. It was many years later, when Gertrude Stein and I had a poodle, that I understood this effort to control their greed.

In Hamburg the Polish governess and I said a tearful farewell, for my parents were taking me back to America on the same boat that had brought us. General Lew Wallace, the first of my authors, was on board. He had been our ambassador to Turkey and had written *Ben Hur*. He gave me an inscribed copy.

Soon after we returned to San Francisco, I was sent to Miss Mary West's school. A little girl in my class asked me if my father was a millionaire. I said I did not know. Had we a yacht? she continued. When she learned we hadn't, she lost interest. My mother said it was time to send me to another school where the little girls would be less snobbish.

The new school, Miss Lake's, was a gay happy one. At once I formed a close friendship with a radiant, resilient, brilliant little girl, Clara Moore, which was to last until her death only a few years ago. After school hours we read the same books, the stories of Juliana Ewing and Louisa Alcott, a sordid dull English novel, *The Lamplighter,* by Miss Cummins, and a story "Honor Bright" that I tried unsuccessfully many years later to find for Gertrude Stein. Then we read Dickens, commencing with *David Copperfield*. I preferred *A Tale of Two Cities* and *Great Expectations*.

My mother gave me a membership card to the Mercantile and Mechanics Library where novels were soon replaced by biographies and memoirs, and at home I had Shakespeare and some poetry.

I remained at Miss Lake's School for four years. Then my father decided we would go to Seattle to live. Two fires and the collapse of a boom had reduced his income seriously, and he hoped to extricate himself from these difficulties there. After we had moved, a committee of San Francisco bankers came to investigate the financial situation in the Northwest. One of them asked my uncle in Spokane how his mining stock was getting on. Very nice and quiet, I thank you, my uncle, not a great talker, replied.

That autumn, I went to Miss Mary Cochrane's School. She and her two sisters were the staff, and all these three knew was what they taught us. They were from the Shenandoah Valley and remembered the Civil War, which was the occasion of considerable bitterness between the Misses Cochrane and their Northern pupils.

While I was at Miss Cochrane's School, Coxey's Army was marching on Washington. My father was one of a committee who tried to keep the men on their farms by giving them implements and maintaining prices for their harvests.

My mother was an ardent gardener, and she planted around the house on a hilltop where we lived small beds of many different flowers. She liked making bouquets with original combinations, particularly Homer roses and hops. In the small beds, with only room between them to weed and to gather the blooms, were all the different flowers she preferred, dwarf yellow pansies and periwinkles and many kinds of sweet peas. I once said to her, You have such lovely watery periwinkle blue eyes. You mean, dearest, liquid eyes, she corrected. The flowers filled the house with their perfume and color.

One autumn we stayed at a hop ranch in the Snoqualmie Valley for several weeks. A young squaw came and asked us for a pair of shoes in which to bury her child who had always gone barefoot. A beautiful Southern girl who was staying at the ranch gave her a pair of very high-heeled white satin slippers.

My mother and little brother spent a few weeks every year with my grandfather in San Francisco. I followed during my vacation. When I was there one year I received a wire from my mother saying that the Misses Cochrane were giving up their school and I should see Miss Sarah Hamlin at once. She would coach me to pass the entrance examinations at the university. Sarah Hamlin had brought the Pundita Ramabei to the United States to lecture against the sacrifice of young Hindu widows on the funeral pyres of their husbands. Every morning at eight o'clock she put me through a course of algebra and trigonometry, sufficient for her to be able to recommend me to the University of Washington.

The winter at the university was a lively one. There were new friends, there were dances and parties on the lake when the weather permitted. It would have been a happy year if my mother's health had not worried us.

The next spring she had an unsuccessful operation. My father decided we should return to San Francisco, where surgeons could be consulted. The furniture was packed, my mother, my father and I and my little brother, my mother's trained nurse and my father's hunting dog took the train. We found a house, a simple home where we were comfortable.

Another operation advised by the best surgeons was not successful and my mother was never strong again. One of her uncles called for us frequently to drive us through Golden Gate Park to the Cliff House. This became too great an exertion for my mother, and the following spring she died. It was a terrible blow for us.

My grandfather persuaded us to move to his home where he lived with his brother Mark and where the house was frequently filled with the cousins from the San Joaquin Valley. The Spanish-American War broke out soon after we moved. As the troops marched down Van Ness Avenue from the Presidio on their way to embark for the Philippines, I could hear their bugles. I would hurry up Van Ness Avenue to say good-bye to the soldiers of the Washington and California regiments. They were the boys with whom I had danced. They were very young and cheerful, very unlike the soldiers of the two World Wars. Those from the San Joaquin Valley would get leave to have a meal with us. The cook and I made great quantities of doughnuts for them to take back to distribute in camp.

My grandfather took me to Southern California to meet his friends of the pioneer days. We went by carriage, by buckboard, by horseback and by muleback. It was amusing but fatiguing. My grandfather, however, was never fatigued. Upon our return at Thanksgiving, we went to the San Joaquin Valley to look at his land.

I had received a parchment certifying me as a bachelor of music. Now I commenced to study piano with Otto Bendix, a pupil of Liszt, and harmony with Oscar Weil. A talented and lovely pupil of theirs, Elizabeth Hansen, became my friend.

Mrs. Moore and her children, who had gone to Europe, now returned. When Clare was preparing for college a tragedy occurred. Jeannie, the second daughter, was burned to death. Her lace dress caught fire in the candles on her dressing table and it was too late before help came. Jeannie had been beautiful, charming, fascinating. Mrs. Moore was prostrate, and Clare became the head of the family. Not long after this they went to Europe again.

I went on with my piano lessons with Otto Bendix. I went to Seattle where Elizabeth Hansen lived and where she and I gave a concert. It was a quite ambitious program of which I only remember that we played Schumann's variations for two pianos. Upon my return to San Francisco I played the Schubert *Wanderer* with orchestra. Soon after that, Otto Bendix died and my musical career came to an end.

My grandfather caught cold, which developed into influenza, and within a week he died. In his will he left a quarter of his estate to my aunt and a quarter to each of his three grandchildren. My father proposed that we should go south for a rest, and close up the big house and move to a smaller one upon our return. We found a pleasant house overlooking the Presidio.

It was an agreeable life. I saw a great deal of Clare's friend Eleanor Joseph. She had a caustic wit and had said of an old classmate, He said, 'Come into the garden, Maud,' and Maud went. I nicknamed her California Nell, and I called her Nellie.

Harriet Levy, who had lived next door to us on O'Farrell Street, returned from Europe where, in Florence, she had met Gertrude Stein and Gertrude's brother Leo. Both were interested in painting. Charles Loeser had introduced them to the pictures of Cézanne. Leo planned to go to Paris to paint, where

Gertrude and he would begin to collect pictures. Gertrude Stein went often to the Pitti and Uffizi galleries, and in the heat of the summer would fall asleep stretched out on one of the benches. She said it was pleasant to wake up with the pictures about her.

In Egypt Harriet had met at a dinner party an Englishman who asked her, Tell me, how much do you pay now to kill a Chinaman in California? Harriet was aghast. I never heard of such a thing, she said. You pay ten dollars to shoot a Chinaman in San Jose, said the Englishman.

The Moores returned again from Europe. Paula, the oldest daughter, did not return with them. She had married a Dr. Wicksteed in London. When he and his brothers were still little boys someone drove up to them while they were walking in the garden and asked them, Does Mr. Wicksteed live here? They answered in chorus, We are the Mr. Wicksteeds.

To have a man at the head of the family, Clare had married William de Gruchy, a French-Canadian raised in Boston, who had settled in San Francisco.

Life went on calmly until one morning we and our home were violently shaken by an earthquake. Gas was escaping. I hurried to my father's bedroom, pulled up the shades, pulled back the curtains and opened the windows. My father was apparently asleep. Do get up, I said to him. The city is on fire. That, said he with his usual calm, will give us a black eye in the East.

Our servant was heating water in the kitchen on an alcohol stove to make coffee. The chimneys had fallen, the pipes were disrupted, there would be no baths. I walked up the hill to the entrance of the Presidio, where in the early morning light General Funston was marching his troops into the city where fires were commencing to burn.

My father, who had at last risen, walked down to the business quarter to see if the vaults of his bank were holding. Convinced that they were, he returned with four hundred cigarettes, all he could find. For Nellie, for Clare and for you, he explained.

I sent the servant to buy such provisions as she could find and I went to see how Nellie had fared. Her two Chinese servants were cooking on an improvised stove on the street. Nellie, with some novels, was distracting her mind as usual in her darkened library.

When I got home, Clare and Harriet were there. After a picnic lunch on the sidewalk, Clare left to join her mother and brother in Sausalito and Harriet went over to Oakland.

Paul Cowles of the Associated Press had met newspapermen at noon at the Fairmount Hotel on Nob Hill. They had asked him if they should meet there again tomorrow. To which Paul replied, If there is a tomorrow.

In the afternoon I packed the family silver in a Chinese chest and had my brother dig a deep hole in the garden into which we put it. The chest we covered with enough earth to protect the silver in case the fire spread. Working on the ground I felt slight tremors from time to time.

My father and brother arranged to spend the night in the nearby Presidio and I was to pass the night with some friends of a woman I knew, in Berkeley. There were no lights, and it was a long and difficult walk to the ferry.

The city was in darkness when we got to the ferry building. I asked if the trains were running on the other side of the bay. Sure, a voice answered from the darkness. People were herded onto the ferry, but there was no confusion. I fortunately was unable to look back upon burning San Francisco from the crowded boat.

At Berkeley there was still a long climb up the hill to the home of the Sidney Armers where they welcomed us, gave us a hot meal and comfortable beds. I slept fitfully and woke early. The Berkeley newspapers were alarming. There was no wire or telephone communication with San Francisco so I went back to San Francisco at once, leaving my friend to be cared for by the Armers.

The crossing, both by train and boat, was more normal than the night before. Passengers were not herded. The Portuguese musicians on the ferry were playing their usual diverting music. I met two of my former teachers from Miss Lake's School, hurrying back to see what remained of their little home.

The city was still burning. The water front and all the way to Van Ness Avenue was in ruins. People would advise one on where it was easiest and safest to walk, yet it took over an hour to get to the house.

My father and brother had not remained long in the Presidio. It seemed safer for one's possessions to remain with them, so they had returned home.

After a cold water sponge I went off again. Passing Annie Fabian's I stopped to ask how they had fared. She was a great carnation specialist and had created many new varieties. The heat of the flames was forcing her many thousands of plants into quicker blooming than a hothouse. Annie could not keep up with the necessary budding and told me I might gather as many as I could carry, which I did to take to Nellie.

Nellie, her sister, her two brothers, Clare, and Frank Jacot, whom Nellie was later to marry, were there. Nellie's oldest brother, who had managed their mother's estate, was depressed. Their income had disappeared in the fire. Nothing but their home remained. It was impossible for the four of them to live on its rent.

Over in Sausalito Clare had found a couple of packages of Venus de Milo cigarettes, which we naturally had never smoked. Then I produced several packages of my father's contribution, which we were pleased to have.

Nellie's Chinese cook prepared an excellent lunch for us. It was not until some weeks later that he told Nellie some thirty cousins of his had come up as refugees from their burning homes in Chinatown. He had gotten sacks of rice and dried Chinese food for them and had put them, the cousins and the food, into Nellie's basement where they lived so quietly for several weeks that no one in the house suspected their presence.

When I returned home my father told me that our landlord had made arrangements with working men to repair the chimneys within a few days, but it would be a while longer before the water mains would be repaired.

I got to work with the servant to clean the house. It was black with soot from the flames. In cleaning a drawer I found two tickets for the performance Sarah Bernhardt was to give of *Phèdre* at the Greek amphitheatre at the University of California. I had forgotten about that. I would go over to Oakland, have a bite and a bath at Harriet's sister's and take her niece with me for the performance. I could not decide whether the performance or the bath was the most alluring.

Bernhardt's voice was as exciting as I remembered it from my youth. On that day there was an especial example. Alone on the stage at the end of the first act, Phèdre gives an anguished cry as she disappears. Evidently Bernhardt had had no rehearsals, nor had she studied the large stage. Her arms outstretched, with her piercing cry she backed forever towards the curtained door. She prolonged the cry, the golden voice continued. The audience was breathless. Finally she reached the curtain and disappeared. I had seen her in many of her poignant roles but was never more moved than then.

After the performance, by great good luck we were near Bernhardt when she was getting into an open barouche in which she was to be driven away. The students from the university had unhitched the horses and were going to draw her. She fearlessly faced the California sun, her head thrown back with her famous radiant smile. I noticed, however, her visibly large teeth.

Life with chimneys and water mains finally repaired seemed normal, though of course it was far from being so. Nellie as usual sat a great part of the day in the darkened library. She was selecting the books she would sell.

Clare and her husband took a flat on Pacific Avenue beyond the fire area. We were all living in an extravagant and at the same time economical way. Later Frank Jacot called us The Necessary Luxury Company. We went to theatres, we went automobiling, we went to the Little Palace Café and Hotel which had become a fashionable shopping district where one could buy Paris clothes and perfume if one could afford it, and even if one could not.

The Michael Steins—Gertrude's elder brother and his wife— had hurried out to San Francisco from Paris to see what repairs would be necessary to their income-bearing flats. They had brought with them the "Portrait à la Raie Verte," of Madame Matisse with a green line down her face. It and the other paintings they brought were the first by Matisse to cross the Atlantic. The portrait impressed me immensely, as "La Femme au Chapeau" had impressed Gertrude Stein when she saw it at the vernissage of the Salon d'Automne of 1905 and bought it at once.

Mrs. Michael Stein followed Gertrude Stein's purchases but did not like the Picasso pictures. Neither did Matisse. Neither the subjects nor the paintings were to his taste. Mrs. Stein followed Matisse blindly. Mr. Stein believed in his wife and whatever she believed in.

Mr. Stein was a gentle creature. One day I was wearing a silver South Sea Island belt with a blue stone in its clasp. When Mike Stein's eye caught the blue stone, he brought from his pocket a small magnifying glass. Examining the stone he said, Ancient Asiatic glass.

My father met me walking with the Steins on Van Ness Avenue one afternoon. At home later he asked me, with all a Pole's prejudice, Who did you say was the German memorial monument you were with today?

Mrs. Stein wanted me to return to Paris with them when she heard from Harriet Levy that some day she and I would go together. I was cool about accepting this invitation, so they compromised with a more accommodating and charming young girl.

Harriet had often spoken of our going to Paris. It was time now to speak to my father about our plans. On the day I did, his first response was a noncommittal sigh. He would close the house and move to his club, he finally said. My brother could live in Berkeley for his two remaining years at the University of California.

We did not get off until September, 1907. It was hot crossing the continent, and while the porter was cleaning our compartment Harriet and I sat in a car where Harriet and the head of the Psychology Department at the University of Edinburgh got into conversation. Thereafter they had long conversations together.

In New York we stayed at an agreeable hotel where Lillian Russell was dining at a roof garden where we dined.

Nellie had by now married Frank Jacot and they were already in New York. Nellie took me the next afternoon to see Nazimova in *A Doll's House*. Her Slav temperament did not suit the role of Nora. It was the last performance of Ibsen I was ever to see.

The next day we drove down to the steamer past the enormous excavations where myriads of men were working and which were to become Grand Central Terminal. It was quite biblical.

Nellie had sent flowers, books, magazines and fruit to the steamer for the voyage. I had Flaubert's letters, and Harriet had a copy of *Lord Jim* that she considered a tactless choice by the friend who had sent it.

On board was a distinguished oldish man, a commodore, who got into conversation with me when I was reading on the deck after lunch. We spent the greater part of the voyage together. Harriet did not speak to me of the episode but I could see that she considered that I lacked discretion. The commodore and I said a calm good-bye before we got on the launches that were taking us into the harbor of Cherbourg.

We were indeed in France. It was a fête day and there was

dancing in the open air. We decided not to take the crowded boat train in the heat of the day but to stay the night in Cherbourg and take a morning train to Paris. Under the hotel window French voices were singing French songs in the mild French air.

2

WHEN I woke up I opened the shutters and leaned out the window while I waited for coffee. Down in the square, men with strange brooms and buckets of water were cleaning up. It was more like a household cleaning than the street cleaning of San Francisco.

The train, when we had boarded it, started with a jerk. We had window seats, and the conductor said that there was a dining car and two seats there were being reserved for us.

The landscape was ravishing, with red poppies, white mar-

guerites and blue cornflowers in the fields and a heavenly blue
sky over all. Miniature villages, houses crowded one next to the
other, a church, cows in the fields, oxen dragging earth – I was
so grateful for it all. Harriet dozed. In the afternoon, having
left Normandy behind, the conductor came to take part of our
tickets and to say we would be in Paris in half an hour.

The station was busier and noisier than any I had ever
known. People were getting off and on, hurrying to the right
and to the left. It took me a long time to become accustomed to
French confusion.

We decided, after we had gotten our baggage through the
customs, to take two fiacres instead of a large closed convey-
ance so that we could see Paris on our way to the hotel. Nellie
had recommended the Magellan, which was near the Etoile
and not far from the avenue du Bois de Boulogne. Its restaurant was well known and excellent. The rooms were very
large – a bedroom, bathroom and dressing room for each of us.
Harriet came in to my room soon after we got there to say she
had telephoned the Mike Steins that we had arrived and were
coming over to see them at once.

Once more we were in those amusing fiacres. The streets
were unlike one another, one quarter did not resemble another,
in fact one house did not have the same character as those on
either side of it. A fine dwelling might have as neighbors a pro-
vision shop, a cleaner. One was not required to leave one's
quarter for shopping in those days. There were many fine
florists and flower markets and a great deal to learn.

The Michael Steins were living then and for some years after
in the rue Madame, in a building built and occupied by a
Protestant church. Their enormous living room had been the
assembly and Sunday school room. It was lighted on one side

by large windows which gave on a garden. On the walls were many pictures.

In the room were Mr. and Mrs. Stein and Gertrude Stein. It was Gertrude Stein who held my complete attention, as she did for all the many years I knew her until her death, and all these empty ones since then. She was a golden brown presence, burned by the Tuscan sun and with a golden glint in her warm brown hair. She was dressed in a warm brown corduroy suit. She wore a large round coral brooch and when she talked, very little, or laughed, a good deal, I thought her voice came from this brooch. It was unlike anyone else's voice – deep, full, velvety like a great contralto's, like two voices. She was large and heavy with delicate small hands and a beautifully modeled and unique head. It was often compared to a Roman emperor's, but later Donald Sutherland said that her eyes made her a primitive Greek.

We were given tea and left shortly afterwards. Gertrude Stein asked me to come to the rue de Fleurus the next afternoon, when she would take me for a walk.

My head was turning with the day's events. After an exquisite dinner I found a book but soon fell asleep. The next morning I unpacked. Harriet thought she would like to lunch in one of the open-air restaurants in the Bois de Boulogne. In which event it would be wise to send word by petit bleu to Gertrude Stein and make my excuses in case I was late. I was by half an hour.

When I got to the rue de Fleurus and knocked on the very large studio door in the court, it was Gertrude Stein who opened it. She was very different from the day before. She had my petit bleu in her hand. She had not her smiling countenance of the day before. She was now a vengeful goddess and I was

afraid. I did not know what had happened or what was going
to happen.

Nor is it possible for me to tell about it now. After she had
paced for some time about the long Florentine table made
longer by being flanked on either side by two smaller ones, she
stood in front of me and said, Now you understand. It is over.
It is not too late to go for a walk. You can look at the pictures
while I change my clothes.

The studio walls were covered from *cimaise* to ceiling with
pictures. The furniture and objects fascinated me. The big
Tuscan table is opposite me as I sit here now, and the rare
octagonal Tuscan table with the three heavy clawed legs is in
the dining room, as well as the double-decked Henry IV buffet
with its three carved eagles on the top. It was only after wip-
ing these and other pieces of furniture that I fully appreciated
their beauty, their details, their proportions. In the room here
at the rue Christine there are only a few objects remaining that
were then at the rue de Fleurus, seventeenth-century terra-
cotta figures of women and several other pieces of Italian pot-
tery.

By the time I had noticed the objects and pieces of furniture,
Gertrude Stein had returned to the studio, more like she had
been the day before. A smile had broken through the gloom
and she laughed again from her brooch. She asked about Harriet, her health, spirits and wit, speaking of her familiarly as
Harriet. Then Gertrude Stein and I took our first walk. In the
nearby Luxembourg Gardens she called my attention. Alice,
she said, look at the autumn herbaceous border. But I did not
propose to reciprocate the familiarity.

The Luxembourg was filled with children around the artificial lake floating their boats; others were rolling hoops with

bells as I had in the Parc Monceau when I was a child. The nurses were still wearing their long capes and starched white caps with long broad streamers. Through the gardens into the Petit Luxembourg and down the boulevard Saint-Michel Gertrude Stein led me, asking me what books I had read on the steamer and were the Flaubert letters translated into English. She did not like to read or speak anything but English, although she knew German and French.

There were students wearing the colored ribbons indicating which school they belonged to at the Sorbonne. Gertrude Stein said there was a good pastry shop where the cakes and ices were the best on the Left Bank, should we not have something there. Which we did, a praline ice, just like San Francisco. While we were having an ice and some cake at a table on the sidewalk, Gertrude Stein said Harriet and I should dine with her and her brother Saturday evening and meet the painters who would come in the evening.

Opposite on the boulevard Saint-Michel was a line of fiacres, and I took one back to the Magellan. Harriet wanted to know how I had enjoyed the walk. I told her only of the walk and nothing of what had occurred before. She remarked, Just as I thought, and was satisfied.

The next morning, on going over to the Right Bank to draw on my letter of credit at my bank in the Place Vendôme and collect any mail that might be there, I found a most compromising letter from the commodore. There was no question of my answering it. I carried it in my handbag into the Tuileries Gardens where I sat down near the artificial lake and tore the letter into shreds, hoping when I dropped them into the lake that no one was seeing me do so. I then walked up the Champs Elysées to the hotel. Well, that episode was closed.

I took to walking mornings and afternoons in all directions and found Paris more and more enchanting. I had not gone to the Louvre, nor would I until the following week. I must first become familiar with what was to be my home town.

Saturday I knocked at the studio door. It was not Gertrude Stein who opened it but her brother Leo, not that I would have recognized him by his resemblance to Gertrude Stein. They did not look at all alike. Gertrude Stein looked like her father's family. The two brothers looked like each other. Like Gertrude Stein, Leo was golden, he had a golden beard. Edith Sitwell told me that when her father had been asked if she resembled him he had answered, Yes, but she has not got this, grasping his beard. Like Gertrude Stein, Leo was clothed in warm brown. They both wore sandals made in Florence from a model Raymond Duncan had designed from those he had seen on a Greek vase in the British museum. Leo had a beautiful springing step and carried his tall body with incomparable grace. He at this time was amiable. But later, when he and Gertrude Stein disagreed about Picasso's pictures and her writing, he became unreasonable and unbearable.

In the studio with the two Steins there was a small, very dark and extremely lively young man, Alfred Maurer, an American painter known to his intimates as Alfy. He was gay and witty, and enjoyed shocking his friends. When he was a guest of the Steins at Fiesole, one evening as he was hanging over the terrace looking down at the Arno Valley he sighed, There should be ten thousand houris there. But ten thousand are a great many, Gertrude Stein said. Not for me, said Alfy.

Hélène, the servant, knocked vigorously on the door and announced dinner. Gertrude Stein led us from the studio, locking the door with an American Yale key. The pavillon door close by was open. The first door to the right in the narrow hallway was the dining room. It was small and made smaller by the book shelves on one of its walls. The two double doors facing each other were lined with Picasso water colors and drawings.

As we were sitting down at table there was a loud knocking at the pavillon door. Hélène came to announce, Monsieur Picasso and Madame Fernande, who in an instant came in, much flustered, both of them talking at the same time. Picasso, very dark with black hair, a lock hanging over one of his marvelous all-seeing brilliant black eyes, was explaining in his raucous Spanish voice, You know how as a Spaniard I would want to be on time, how I always am. Fernande, with her characteristic gesture of one arm extended above her head with a Napoleonic forefinger pointing in the air, asked Gertrude Stein to excuse them. The new suit she was wearing, made for the next day's vernissage of the Salon d'Automne, had not been delivered on time and there was of course nothing to do but wait. Fernande was a large heavy woman with the sensational natural coloring of a *maquillage,* her dark eyes were narrow slits. She was an oriental odalisque. The attention she was attracting pleased her and she sat down satisfied.

The dinner was simple but well cooked. Hélène did not know how or like to cook complicated dishes, nor those that took a long time to prepare. She would not consider preparing those delicious French crêpes. But her roasting was perfection. A leg of mutton invariably was a rare treat. She would put it in the oven, go out on an errand in the neighborhood, and would return at the right moment to baste it.

Conversation at table was lively. While we were still at dessert, Hélène came to say that there were guests in the studio.

Gertrude Stein left the dining room hurriedly. We followed soon after to find her sitting in a high leather Tuscan Renaissance armchair, her feet resting on several saddle bags piled on one another.

She introduced a good looking red-haired man, Pierre Roché, who spoke a smattering of several languages including Hungarian; Hans Purrmann, a German painter devoted to Matisse; Patrick Henry Bruce, who with Mrs. Michael Stein had persuaded Matisse to open his school; Sayen, who had been an electrical prodigy at the Thomson-Houston Company but had given it up to come to Paris to paint; a group of Montmartrois who surrounded Picasso like the cuadrilla does a bullfighter; Braque; and Chremnitz, who could sing "The Old Kent Road" with a marked French accent. Also there were Apollinaire, the Spanish painter Pichot, and the false Greco who made jewelry.

Fernande and Braque were playing at being *des incroyables*. I had thought he was an American. A real American was William Cook, who had painted the portraits of the English duchesses and later of the Roman world, including a number of cardinals, but had given this up and had betaken himself to etching.

By the time Harriet had spoken to everyone whom Gertrude Stein had introduced to her and some whom she had not, Harriet was ready to leave. Gertrude Stein made an appointment to meet us the next afternoon at the vernissage of the Salon d'Automne. She asked me if I would like to take French lessons from Fernande, who had been well educated and had read aloud La Fontaine's fables while Picasso was painting Gertrude Stein's portrait.

We got to the vernissage early and had no difficulty in finding the *salle des fauves,* wild animals, as they were called. Picasso was surrounded by his cuadrilla excepting Braque, who was serving a double allegiance; he was of the group about Fernande.

When Fernande noticed Harriet and me she came over in her ponderous way to speak to us and to introduce her friends, Alice Derain whose calm beauty had given her the nickname of *La Vierge* and Germaine Pichot whose looks were quite the opposite.

I spoke to Fernande about wanting to take French lessons. Would she come to the hotel in the morning to give them there? She called me Mees (Miss) Toklas and said she would ask two francs fifty an hour, fifty cents. I said I would wish to pay her cabs. Oh no, she laughed, I shall take the bus or the metro. We set a day for the following week. Gertrude Stein came up. She spoke to the three Montmartrois and then wanted to know if the lessons had been arranged. The mornings, I said, she will come at ten and stay until one.

The room commenced to be crowded. There were not only French but Russians, a few Americans, Hungarians and Germans. The discussions were lively but not entirely friendly. A very small Russian girl was holding forth explaining her picture, a nude holding aloft a severed leg. It was the beginning of the Russian horrors. She was a student at the Matisse school. The first day Matisse came to criticize the pictures he had asked her, as was his habit, For what are you striving, mademoiselle? She had answered, without a moment's hesitation, The modern, the new. The class applauded.

Picasso came to speak to us. You are taking lessons from Fernande, he said to me. She is highly educated, he said with an unflattering implication, she is bored, do not allow that to become contagious. Gertrude must bring you to see me. I too live in Montmartre, he said with his laugh like a young colt.

The next week the Mike Steins asked us to lunch with them. There was a postscript in Mike's handwriting. After lunch, he said, I shall take Alice to the Louvre. It is scandalous that she has not yet found time to go there. I thought she was interested in pictures. Perhaps I was but perhaps it was not my major interest.

Lunch was served in the living room. Allan, the little son of the Steins, was present. His mother, when she was conscious of him, coddled him; his father was more thoughtful of what would please a child. Both Matisse and Picasso had painted portraits of him, the greatest distinction he was to know.

After lunch Mike and I walked to the river, crossed the foot bridge and were quickly in the Louvre at the foot of the "Victory of Samothrace." Mike quickly led me up the steep flight of stairs to the Salle Carré. It was a gorgeous surprise but only a moment was allowed me before Giorgione's "La Fête Champêtre." Down the long gallery I was rushed. So that you may know where to find things, explained Mike as we hurried past miles of pictures. I was exhausted.

Mike then took me across to the rue de Rivoli, where we had an ice at an incomparable Hungarian pastry shop.

We two Californians, Harriet and I, had commenced to feel that we needed a more homelike dwelling. Harriet suggested a furnished flat. In the *Figaro* I found a discreet advertisement, a Count de C. wished to rent a floor in his home suitable for two people. Harriet was less hopeful than I but said to investigate it at once.

After lunch I went over to the rue de la Faisanderie. It was a small stone house. The door was opened by a very correct butler who led me to a salon furnished with eighteenth-century furniture and a grand piano. There were several vases with fine hothouse flowers. Almost at once a young man came into the room introducing himself, Monsieur de Courcy. He spoke in English, Oxford English. It is about the flat you have come, he said. It is a floor of three rooms and bath. He thought it would be suitable for two ladies.

There was a narrow flight of stairs leading to the next floor, which consisted of a salon less elaborate than the room below, but well furnished in the same taste, with a telephone, and two bedrooms facing on a small court where there was a stable with a coachman washing a coupé. Monsieur de Courcy showed me the bathroom which separated the bedrooms. We then returned to the salon on the first floor and I asked what he was asking for the floor he had just shown me. He wanted to know at what hotel we were staying and what we were paying there. Because, he explained, I shall expect you to pay me one-third less. That, I told him, would be satisfactory, if the cooking was. Oh, said Monsieur de Courcy, my mother who by the way is paying a short visit to friends in the Loire is a great gourmet. We have an excellent cook and this is a good marketing district. So I made an appointment for the next morning to bring my friend to see the rooms. Upon which I bade him good-bye and hurried back to the Magellan to tell Harriet of what I believed was a discovery.

Harriet was surprised and pleased. The next morning, very early, we went over to the rue de la Faisanderie. The rooms we were to have were filled with lovely flowers. The bathroom was supplied with a quantity of towels. Harriet was enchanted with everything and asked if we could move the next day.

Come in time for lunch, said Monsieur de Courcy, at one o'clock.

Back at the Magellan we told the secretary of our plan. She amiably said the maid would help us pack. Harriet had a great number of cardboard boxes, for sewing and writing material, for jewelry, for toilet articles, which she proceeded to pack and make secure with rubber bands.

We moved to the rue de la Faisanderie, our new home, the next morning in time to get some unpacking done before lunch was announced. The cook was indeed excellent. The table was set with heavy silver and cut glass. Lunch commenced with a mixed shellfish salad, followed by breaded lamb chops with fresh green peas and for dessert a wild strawberry ice. A delicious white wine from the property of their friends in the Loire accompanied the lunch. Coffee was served in the salon. Monsieur de Courcy asked if either of us were musicians. He asked, Would you like me to play some Chopin for you? He played some of the études with a good technique and interesting interpretation.

Our host wanted to know if we would care to go to the Folies Bergère that evening. Harriet said she would prefer to postpone it to the next evening. She said if it would be convenient we would like a light supper, a cup of bouillon, a vegetable and a compôt or fresh fruit, to be served in our sitting room.

I wrote some letters, and a note to Gertrude Stein to tell her of our find, asking her to lunch with us on the day that would suit her. At supper in our sitting room Harriet and I felicitated each other on our fortunate situation.

The following morning we took a fiacre and drove around the Bois, down to the cascade, to the river around the race track, to Pré-Catalan and back to the flat. Monsieur de Courcy said he would telephone to the Folies Bergère for seats for that evening.

After lunch Harriet rested and I took a walk down the avenue Victor Hugo to look at the shop windows, returning in time for dinner and to dress. The performance at the Folies Bergère was elaborately staged and what was not understood was happily not understood. The audience was of all nationalities. In the foyer during the intermission the young women, dressed to attract the attention of men, were sauntering singly and in couples. One of them hearing us speak English said, I speak English too. Monsieur de Courcy was not embarrassed. After the performance was over our young host took us for supper to Paillard. Harriet was exhausted. The next day at lunch Monsieur de Courcy suggested we go that evening to the Comédie Française but we both demurred and said we would skip an evening. Which we did. Then we went to a classic performance of *Ruy Blas* with Mounet Sulley.

Gertrude Stein came over for lunch and she put the end to our life in the flat. She considered the continued absence of Madame de Courcy explainable only on the ground that she had never been informed that Harriet and I were her son's boarders in her home, that we should at the end of the week leave the flat before any new complications arose. Find a hotel in our quarter at once and move over, she said. If you have any trouble, but I do not think you will, send me a petit bleu.

So we again commenced to pack, and at dinner we told Monsieur de Courcy. Poor young man. He kept repeating, But I thought you were pleased here, quite content – indeed happy – with everything. My mother will be disappointed at not finding you here upon her return. What shall I say to her? To which Harriet maintained a smiling silence. Harriet and I had agreed to make no explanation. Not one of the three of us was free in expressing our feelings. After dinner we excused ourselves to finish our packing. It was a very different departure from our arrival.

The next morning we said a perhaps too gay farewell to Monsieur de Courcy. In the meantime a petit bleu from Gertrude Stein had come saying we should try the Hotel de l'Univers on the boulevard Saint-Michel. So we drove over there.

The hotel was pleasantly situated between the garden of the Petit Luxembourg and the garden of the Deaf and Dumb Institute. Strindberg had stayed at the hotel. Harriet was to have a large room with windows facing the Petit Luxembourg, and I a small one facing the garden of the Institute. Baths were in a bathroom apart.

By the time we commenced to unpack and the rooms were in a great mess, Gertrude Stein arrived with a little bouquet for Harriet and some chocolates for me. She said at once she thought we had made a wise change. At any rate an economical one, for the hotel was charging almost half the price of the flat, nearly a quarter of the Magellan, and it was about twenty minutes walk across the Luxembourg Gardens to 27 rue de Fleurus. Gertrude Stein and I could go places together and take walks.

It was the beginning of my friendship with Gertrude Stein and I was to call her Gertrude. I never did get to calling Mrs. Michael Stein Sally. Sarah she remained, but Mike was easy. I saw more of Mike than of Sarah but mostly I saw Gertrude.

Harriet and I went to Saturday evenings at the rue de Fleurus. My French lessons with Fernande were held three times a week. As Fernande had small interests in anything beyond clothes and perfumes, I soon came to taking her to shows of paintings and to meeting her friends Alice Derain and Germaine Pichot at her flat in Montmartre. It was elaborately furnished with rented objects, an upright piano, Turkish covers for bed and table, opaque glass bowls and ash trays. It was in wretched taste. I suggested asking Fernande's friends over to the hotel for tea, but Fernande postponed the visit. Gertrude told me that Fernande considered Alice Derain's conversation too frank and not suitable for Harriet. For me it was all right.

Fernande was a difficult companion. She was jealous of other women, of other women's beauty, of the attention they attracted from men. But she went into ecstasies over Evelyn Thaw, who was much in the newspapers at the time and was small, colorless and unimpressive.

Fernande held Pablo by her beauty. Much later when they had separated permanently he said of her, I never liked any of her little ways but her beauty always held me. When she was ill, Pablo paid largely for her care at a smart nursing home and when I went to see her there I was astonished at her beauty.

Fernande told me a great many stories at that time, about Van Dongen, about Germaine Pichot, about Marie Laurencin. Marie Laurencin was in those early days plain. She had protruding near-sighted eyes, prominent thick lips, and temperamentally reminded us of some strange mythological animal. Fernande said Marie made low wild cries like small animals and that Pablo could not tolerate them or her.

Gertrude was eager to know if Fernande was wearing her large Spanish gold hoop earrings. It was some weeks before it was revealed to me what the meaning of this could be. It developed that Fernande had quarreled with Picasso and that now, after a passage of time, she had pawned her earrings.

Which meant that she had no money left and they would soon have a reconciliation.

Fernande gave up her flat and moved back to Picasso's studio in the rue Ravignan. It was then that I took to taking Fernande shopping, to dog and cat shows, to anything that would give her a subject of conversation. Picasso was grateful to me for taking Fernande off his hands.

I saw them Saturday evenings at the rue de Fleurus. And there of all people I met Louise Hayden. Louise had been studying to be a concert pianist in Munich and, having had enough of Munich, came with her mother to Paris to live. They had found a well-heated flat on the boulevard Raspail, and I went up to see them quite frequently. Louise in a short while became one of the favorite pupils of Phillipe, a very well-known teacher and pianist in Paris. Gertrude thought that he had taught her to play too quickly.

Crossing the Luxembourg one day I ran into Leslie Hunter, a San Francisco painter, a large burly Scotchman. He came to see me and took me on long, cold, winter walks and I took him to see the pictures at the rue de Fleurus, which shocked him profoundly. He wished he had never gone to see them. His painting was under the influence of Sir Thomas Lawrence.

It was at this time that a new and alarming development occurred. In San Francisco, Harriet had been under the influence of a Mrs. King, a formidable intellectual married to a High Church curate. Mrs. King had been trying to bring Harriet to a realization of her husband's conception of God. Poor Harriet was tormented, and confessed her troubles to Gertrude. They began to have long conversations. One afternoon Gertrude told Harriet there was nothing for her, Harriet, to do but to kill herself. This upset me more than it did Harriet, who merely retired into a deep silence. Gertrude went home and I went down to dinner. When I returned to my room there was a scrawled note from Harriet on my writing table saying not to wake her in the morning, she would let me know when she was awake. I fell asleep reading one of the thirty volumes of George Sand's life I had found in a second-hand bookshop on the rue de Vaugirard.

It was early when Harriet woke me with a repeated call, Alice come at once. I threw on my dressing gown and hurried into Harriet's room. She was sitting up in bed, her small bright eyes brighter than ever. I have seen God, she said in a hushed voice. He came to me in a drop of water from Heaven. I am so happy for you, I started to say, but she made a gesture to stop me. Go over to Gertrude, she said, and bring her over at once. I must see her without delay.

I dressed and went down to the hotel entrance, where I found a fiacre and had him take me over to the rue de Fleurus and engaged him to wait to take us back to the hotel. I looked at my watch. It was half-past eight. Hélène said Mademoiselle Gertrude was not awake yet, she had orders never to awaken her. But this morning it was urgent. She went upstairs and I heard a violent rapping on the door. Finally Hélène returned to say Mademoiselle was dressing and would come down shortly, she would prepare coffee for us. Kind Hélène.

When Gertrude appeared I told her what had happened. Gertrude let out a large laugh. Harriet preferred seeing God to killing herself. What am I to do with her. We will have to find someone who will undertake a solution of her experience. Perhaps Sally.

When we got to the hotel I let Gertrude go in to talk to Harriet while I bathed, dressed, and had a second coffee.

For the next day or two there were strange evenings and mysterious conversations with Sarah Stein, who was a Christian Scientist. Was Harriet being led to this? Nothing was being confided to me. But on the rare occasions I saw Harriet she was her old self.

During these few days I saw Gertrude, who said Sally would not tolerate her participation in Harriet's salvation. Gertrude said she would not want to participate. So she and I took to walking and going to see paintings.

But Sarah Stein soon decided that Harriet took too much of her time from her painting. Sarah had become the favorite pupil of Matisse at the school she and Patrick Henry Bruce had persuaded him to open. Sarah and Pat had found the studio, a very large one near Matisse's flat and his own studio, which had a rather low rental even for those days. Gertrude always spoke of Matisse as *le cher maître,* in derision of course.

The school was comprised of foreigners – three Americans, some Czechs and young Hungarians, an Italian, and quantities of Germans. Olga Merson, a young and good-looking Russian, attached herself to one after the other of the young men. She was indifferent to their indifference to her charms. Eventually she took an especial interest in the *cher maître.* He was blondish and wore gold spectacles, making him look like a German professor. Was this in memory of her student days in Germany?

There was a great deal of disagreement amongst the students, and a good deal of jealousy of Sarah Stein's intimacy with Matisse as the result of the purchases of his pictures by the Mike Steins. Pat Bruce used to come over to the rue de Fleurus after a short visit to the rue Madame on Saturday evenings. Bruce had a sharp eye and a sharper tongue. He thought

Sarah Stein overdid the admiration of Matisse, as man not as painter, for Bruce was a sincere follower of the Matisse school of paintings. He said about this time that it was not the struggles of the great painters that were pitiable but of the minor painters. Was he not one?

Bruce agreed with the opinion of Matisse concerning Picasso, unsympathetic as a man and less than negligible as a painter. Matisse had said that Gertrude's feeling for Picasso and her visits to the rue Ravignan were for the spectacle that she saw there. Gertrude, hearing this, let out one of her fine large laughs. She was not even angry. But I commenced to have my opinion of *cher maître*.

Sarah Stein now told Gertrude of her giving up the spiritual care of Harriet. They thought David Edstrom should undertake the case. David Edstrom was a good-looking young Swedish sculptor. He had not known anything like Harriet before, though he had known many American women in Florence where he had lived for several years. He soon told Gertrude lively stories of Harriet's spiritual life.

3

___

WHILE I was meeting the ladies of Montmartre, Gertrude was correcting the last proofs of *Three Lives* and working on her monumental book, *The Making of Americans*. She gave me some pages of it to read. This came about when she discovered that her theory of dependent independent and independent dependent natures fascinated me and that I was working on examples of people I knew. She had me tell her what I knew and how I came to know it. It was very exciting, more exciting than anything else had ever been. Even, I said to her laughing, more exciting than Picasso's pictures promise to be.

In the study of character in *The Making of Americans* Gertrude was gradually led to her theory of the two divisions of character in men and women, the independent dependent and the dependent independent, based on what she called their bottom nature. This had to do with resemblance and differences but more particularly with their approaches. "The strongest thing in each one is the bottom nature in them. Other kinds of natures are in almost all men and in almost all women mixed up with the bottom nature in them. Some men have it in them to be attacking. Some men have it in them to be made more or less of the mixing inside them of another nature or of other kinds of nature with the bottom nature of them. There are two kinds of men and women, those who have dependent independent nature in them, those who have independent dependent nature in them. The ones of the first kind of them always somehow own the ones they need to love them, the second kind have it in them to have power in them over others only when these others have begun already a little to love them, others loving them give to such of them strength in domination. Many men and many women have resisting in them. Many men and many women have attacking in them. The nature in every one is always coming out of them from their beginning to the ending by the repeating that is always coming from each one of them. There are then the two kinds of all men and women of all who are or ever will have in them human being, there are then always to my thinking in all of them the two kinds of them, the dependent independent, the independent dependent, the first having resisting as the fighting power in them, the second have attacking as their natural way of fighting.

"Realizing kinds in ways of being, learning in being, thinking to feeling, realizing meaning in being, realizing many kinds of sensitiveness and emotion, meaning of stupidness in being, ways of telling, ways of knowing, ways of being resembling, all these things always are in me filling me with seeing, feeling, learning understanding, filling me sometimes to telling. Some of such of them make of themselves a whole one in themselves and sometimes make of themselves a whole one to others around them. This is very interesting, this is sometimes the explanation of melodrama to some one. Sometimes then each one is a whole one to me, sometimes then each one has a whole history of each one for me. Everything they do then in living is clear then to me, their living, loving, eating, pleasing, smoking, scolding, drinking, dancing, thinking, working, walking, talking, laughing, sleeping, suffering, joking, everything in them. They are whole beings then. They are themselves inside them to me. They are then each one a whole one inside me. Repeating of the whole of them always coming out of each one of them makes history always of each one of them to me."

The Making of Americans, although it was written between 1906 and 1911, was not published until 1925. The characters in *The Making of Americans* were originally the Steins, at their Stratton home in East Oakland, and the servants and people who worked for them.

When Gertrude lectured at Mills College in California in 1935 we tried to find the old Stratton home in East Oakland, but it had been replaced by small houses. Returning to the scenes of her childhood saddened Gertrude.

The Grafton Press had already undertaken to publish *Three Lives,* with Gertrude paying the expenses. After the manuscript had been read by the Grafton Press they had said they would send someone over to talk to her about the book. An American living in Paris came to see her and said he had been asked to correct her book for the Grafton Press. Gertrude said, There is no occasion for correction. He said, They think you are uneducated and that it is necessary to go over it with you, and she said, No, you are mistaken about that, I am not uneducated. I have had more education and experience than they or you. Whereupon he left.

The winter commenced gaily. Gertrude during this winter diagnosed me as an old maid mermaid which I resented, the old maid was bad enough but the mermaid was quite unbearable. I cannot remember how this wore thin and finally blew away entirely. But by the time the buttercups were in bloom, the old maid mermaid had gone into oblivion and I had been gathering wild violets. The lilies of the valley, forget-me-nots and hyacinths we gathered in the forest of Saint-Germain were more delicately colored than those of California, which were more robust and even more fragrant.

In a shop in the rue de Rivoli I found some beautiful faceted raspberry-colored corals from San Francisco, which I bought, intending to give them to Gertrude. But they were insignificant compared to her lapis lazuli Chinese mandarin chain, so I wore them instead. They looked particularly well on my pale gray San Francisco dresses. The day inevitably came when they were given to Harriet. I had lost all interest in them when Mike and Sarah arranged them with rosary beads.

Mike Stein had been making jewelery, chains and brooches in the manner of my corals from San Francisco. He wanted me to sell his jewelry to the people I had been meeting. It was embarrassing for me to accept or to refuse, but fortunately for me the Steins found that a French law would not permit the sale in one's home of objects without declaring the sale and paying a tax to the state. This was too complicated, so the Steins sent their jewelry to the United States or sold it to Americans returning there. That arrangement lasted some years, Mike finding the material and Sarah making the designs.

During the complications of the winter, Ada Joseph descended unexpectedly upon me from London for a short visit. She had brought me a splendid long wide lynx stole and muff, which I wore for many years. Ada wanted to take me to all the restaurants and theatres she knew and we went gaily from one to another, starting with the restaurant Lapérouse. She was wearing English clothes, duchess clothes I called them, and the Parisians were all surprised at her perfect French.

Ada had a lovely smile that won Gertrude. But later, when Ada returned married to Harry Brackett, Gertrude was bored with them. One had to have a special taste for Harry Brackett. Ada could compromise one in an innocent way but there was nothing innocent about the Bracketts.

Ada and I went to the best of the restaurants and the most questionable of the comedies. Ada was more accustomed to them than I. I was shocked. At the first one I proposed leaving the theatre at the end of the first act. Nonsense, said Ada, this is mild.

The food at the restaurants was like the good food in San Francisco at the Palace Hotel, the Poodle Dog and the Pup, where the cooking was in the French manner.

After only a week in Paris, Ada returned to London and I went to the plays of Bernstein in which Guitry père performed. In one of them I saw one of the first portable telephones. Before that, they had always been attached to the wall. The audi-

ence buzzed with excitement as the curtain went up and revealed it. The acting was as brilliant as the lines.

I saw a good many plays, and then the Russian ballet opened
at the Châtelet. One warm evening Harriet and I drove to it
down the boulevard Saint-Michel in an open fiacre. At that first
performance they gave "The Specter of the Rose" to the music
of Weber's "Invitation to the Dance," with Nijinsky making his
long high spectacular leap. The corps de ballet danced in "Les
Sylphides" to a waltz of Chopin in which Olga Khokhlova,
later Picasso's wife, made her debut. It was all ravishing and
breathtaking. Madame Marvel, a painter, came to speak to us,
and she and I between ballets went to the box office to get
tickets for the following night.

Harriet during the winter was seeing nobody who was not a
Christian Scientist, and she went regularly to their meetings
held twice a week near the Etoile. One of her church friends
was a Miss Cora Downer from Kalamazoo, a worldly woman
who dressed well and had a large acquaintance in the fashionable world. During the winter of 1908 the opera of *Boris
Godunov* was given with the great singer Chaliapin. The audience at the first performance to which Harriet and I went was
an exceedingly smart one, and Miss Downer pointed out to us
many of the distinguished people present. The most noticeable
of them was a Pole, wife of an ambassador, an exceptional
beauty wearing a diamond necklace and diamonds in her hair.

When winter passed, it grew hot, then sultry. I spent the
mornings in the arcades of the Odéon looking at and buying
books. Evenings I read them.

One evening the Jacots were to take me to a cabaret. Frank
called for me, Nellie was not feeling well and excused herself.

When Frank and I got to Luigi's Frank said to him, This is a schoolmate of my wife. Ah yes, said Luigi skeptically.

Harriet and I became acquainted with Miss Ethel Mars and Miss Squire, who were Miss Furr and Miss Skeene in Gertrude's story, and with Jo Davidson and his beautiful wife, Yvonne. We were also friendly with Harry Phelan Gibb and Bridget, his pretty wife.

Whether or not Harriet continued to see David Edstrom frequently, I do not recall. But one day Edstrom had a conversation with me. I was leaving the Café de Lillas, where I went once a week to write a long letter to my father. Edstrom came up to me smiling and said, Come back and have a drink with me. I do not drink, I said. I just take enough coffee to cover the use of the table. Well then, may I walk back to the hotel with you? he replied.

As soon as we had crossed the Place de l'Observatoire and gotten into the boulevard Saint-Michel he blurted out, Did you know my wife was in town? As a matter of fact I did not know he had a wife, but to acknowledge this would involve too much time, so I shook my head negatively. I do not want to see her yet, said Edstrom, let me walk with you.

I am scared of her, he went on, evidently very perturbed. Goodness only knows what she would say to me if she met me alone. Maybe she has heard that I want to get a divorce from her. Come on, I said, if you think I am any protection. Yes, yes, breathed Edstrom. I was growing quite attached to silly Edstrom but did not look forward to defending him.

Harriet and Gertrude knew about his wife, Gertrude had met her in Florence. Mrs. Edstrom looked older than Edstrom, she was an intellectual and was quite plain. She wore men's hats, boots, gloves. Her father was the highest magistrate in

Sweden, and he would protect her against any of Edstrom's pranks.

Gertrude thought he would not introduce his wife to Harriet, but we both noticed Harriet was ordering a number of dresses from a dressmaker Nellie had recommended to me.

But the commotion passed, for one morning Gertrude came over to the hotel to tell us that we could have the Casa Ricci at Fiesole for the summer months. Mike had rented the large Villa Bardi for Sarah and himself with Allan and for Leo and Gertrude. That would leave the Casa Ricci free. Harriet and I were overjoyed at the prospect and began at once the necessary preparations for the summer.

We went down to Milan by train in intense heat and spent the night there. The next morning we went on to Florence. Because of the heat I got rid of my cerise ribbon girdle in the dressing room of the train, throwing it out the window. When I returned to our compartment Harriet said, What a strange coincidence, I just saw your cherry-colored corset pass by the window.

From Florence we had a pleasant cool evening's drive to Fiesole, where Gertrude was waiting to meet us.

Gertrude took to coming to the Casa Ricci mornings to call for me to go down with her to Florence to change books at Vieuxsieux's Library and to do my errands. I had boots beautifully made to order, the only luxury I allowed myself – or, rather, Mike allowed me.

Gertrude took me in Florence to lunch with Dr. Claribel and Miss Etta Cone, whom she had known first in Baltimore and then in Paris. Dr. Claribel was handsome and distinguished, Miss Etta not at all so. She and I disagreed about who should pay the lunch bill.

Gertrude also took me to Bernard Berenson's at Settignano where I met his wife Mary, her brother Logan Pearsall Smith and their cousin Emily Dawson, and to meet the Edmund Houghtons who lived in an early fifteenth-century palazzo. She also introduced me to the Algar Thorolds. One of their little daughters said she had blasphemed the saints by permitting her cat to give birth to kittens in their chapel. One day we went to the Boccaccio Villa Gamberaia, owned by Miss Florence Blood and the Princess Ghika. Its wonderful gardens had been restored by Miss Blood. It was while climbing the hill from Settignano to Fiesole that the string of my fine old corals broke. We managed to gather all but one of them.

There are some delightful snapshots of the Steins on the terrace of the Villa Bardi with the Von Heiroths. She was a beautiful blonde Finn married for the third time, he a distinguished Russian who as a young man was quite penniless. He played the piano in a masterly manner and his sister would put money on the piano to pay him for the pleasure he had given her. He was a good fencer and he and Leo fenced together.

The Making of Americans was being written, and Gertrude gave me more of the manuscript to read. Some of Gertrude's friends who came to Fiesole and Florence she used as characters in the book. Amongst the portraits was an extraordinary one of Harriet.

Another was of Gertrude's pretty cousin Bird Gans, Julia Dehning in the book.

Bird Gans was an early social worker, particularly interested in mother classes. She took this very seriously, giving an air of importance to it. Gertrude wrote the papers Mrs. Gans read at their meetings. She was a foolish person with intellectual pretensions. Gertrude said she was a heavy leaner.

One day when Gertrude and I had gone down to Florence we met Thomas Whittemore. He was a friend from Gertrude's early days at Radcliffe. When a great collection of Chinese paintings arrived in Boston at the Museum, Mr. Whittemore had been given the direction of their unpacking and classification which he asked Gertrude to share. It was a pleasure that remained vivid in her memory. They had become intimate friends, calling each other by their Christian names. After the Liberation Gertrude still spoke of him with fondness as Tommy. He came often to the unheated flat, wearing his fur-lined coat and leaning on the small electric radiator whose heat was all we were allowed.

We met him now by accident in Florence. All of a breathless twitter he said, Do you know that *Three Lives* is being published today? Gertrude was rosy with pleasure. We will meet here in an hour, he said. When we did, Mr. Whittemore was waiting with a most exquisite small bouquet which he gave Gertrude, kissing her hand.

Gertrude took me on long walks. My father had taught me to walk in the forests around Seattle and to take the long steps of a tall man. Gertrude was a good walker and loved to walk in the hot Italian sun. When she was tired she stretched out on the ground, looking up at the sun.

Gertrude and I had some unforgettable walks. The two I liked most were pilgrimage walks. The first was to the mountain top where Saint Francis and Saint Dominic met. It was a long climb one blistering hot day. The climb commenced gradually but grew rough, and we slipped on the dry earth. Gertrude took off her sandals, advising me to do the same. The higher we climbed, the finer the view of the valley below became. On the top we were in clouds. After we had rested a little we ate the sandwiches I had brought along. Years later I found in Madrid the two saints, Saint Francis and Saint Dominic, beautifully worked in painted stucco with fine carved gilded frames, which are today on the wall in the entrance of the rue Christine.

The other walk was really a series of walks. We went by railroad to Arezzo to see the pictures, then to Gubbio, Saint Francis' wolf, the most enchanting of the Tuscan hill towns with its wonderful civic and church architecture. We could not tear ourselves away from it, but time was fleeing and we had an appointment with Harriet at Assisi. So we went on by way of Perugia, where we stayed in a hotel that had been a palace and where the sixteenth-century rooms had hunting scenes with the local landscape as background. We went to the museum to see the Fra Angelico paintings. The square overhanging the valley was filled after sunset with glowworms and fireflies and noisy swifts and swallows. We dined at an excellent restaurant where we had perfect scampi and fritto misto.

Then I gave one valise to be sent back to Fiesole and another to Assisi. Gertrude wore a corduroy skirt and a pongee shirtwaist, I a Dutch cotton batik dress, and we walked and walked for hours. The sun was giving a torrid heat, so under some bushes I discarded my silk combination and stockings. It was all I could do.

We now had to make the long part of our climb. We had caught up with some peasant pilgrims from all parts of Italy. Gertrude had a gift for Italian dialects and got to talking to various groups. I did not have the courage to even mingle with them. They were beautiful beyond words but malodorous if one caught nothing more than a whiff. So we took a long breath and got beyond the pilgrims, steadily climbing until still higher the cathedral of Assisi appeared. It was several hours before we were at its doors. I went in for a prayer, and Gertrude went in to look at the great Cimabue. Then we went on to the clean inn at which we were to stay and where Harriet was awaiting us.

In September it was time to think of returning to Paris. I began to gather my handmade shoes together. I had explained to Mike, who was managing my economics, that they were smarter, more comfortable and cheaper than the ready-made ones would be in Paris. Mike permitted me to buy them, and encouraged me to buy a simple Tuscan table, chairs and a credenza. The antique shops in Florence at that time were filled with the most tempting treasures.

By the time we got back to Paris, Harriet and I had decided not to return to the hotel but to find an apartment. We went temporarily to the Hotel des Saints Pères, where the Cone sisters were staying. How we came to find the apartment in the rue Notre Dame des Champs I cannot remember, but it was exactly what we were looking for. The four rooms and kitchen were light and sunny on the first story. There was neither elevator nor bathroom, but the rent was low.

A handsome Renaissance table Harriet had bought was given the place of honor in the sitting room. Harriet also bought some good rugs. I hemstitched mesh curtains, chaste but elegant as the Victorians used to say, and bought some camel's back cushions, now in mothballs in the credenza in the rue Christine.

Then we had to find a servant. Gertrude's concierge recommended his young niece to us. What do I ask her about her cooking? I asked Gertrude. Ask her if she can make an omelette, Gertrude replied. The girl said she could. When she came the next morning ready to commence work I gave her a notebook and pencil, a purse with some change for her marketing, and a basket. But she looked bewildered and said she had never done any marketing, so we went off together. The omelette which was to commence our lunch was burned. It was necessary to tell her uncle that she was not yet sufficiently experienced, and for me to find someone more competent to replace her.

Marie Enz was a typical Swiss old maid, clean, honest, coquettish. She was a plain cook but a good marketer. Gertrude would stay unexpectedly for a meal which at first flurried poor Marie, but she would fly to a good nearby pastry shop for an ice or a tart. She spent the winter with us and then confided to me that she was going to be married in the summer. A white orange blossom wreath and a lace-bordered veil were appropriate gifts from Harriet and me.

Three Lives had begun to receive reviews. I subscribed to Romeike's press-clipping bureau, the advertisements for which I had read years before in the San Francisco *Argonaut*. An intelligent and warm criticism in the Kansas City *Star* surprised and pleased us, surprised us because we had not known of the newspaper's existence. Those were proud and happy days when we received the first clippings.

The few friends to whom Gertrude had sent copies wrote warmly. Georgiana King of Bryn Mawr, an old friend from Baltimore, not only wrote enthusiastically but from that time introduced Gertrude's work in her lectures. Gertrude had also sent a copy to H. G. Wells. He thanked her, much later, in a short but appreciative letter which touched her. It is now in the Gertrude Stein Collection at Yale University.

I had commenced the typewriting of *The Making of Americans* on a worn out little Blickensdorfer. Gertrude decided we should have a proper machine, and Frank Jacot recommended that we buy a Smith Premier. We ordered one. It was a formidable affair. There were a great many appliances removed by an imposing personage who had delivered the machine. He put them in his bag, and I was surprised that they were not deducted from the bill.

Then I commenced to teach myself to become an efficient typist and gradually achieved a professional accuracy and speed. I got a Gertrude Stein technique, like playing Bach. My fingers were adapted only to Gertrude's work. Later, when we published the Plain Edition, writing business letters proved difficult. My own typing had to be done by a friend or professionally. After Gertrude died, my typewriter remained unused and I gave it to a young boy.

I went over to the rue de Fleurus and did the typewriting mornings, before Gertrude came down. She was at that time a very late riser. She had her breakfast coffee at the lunch table at one o'clock.

Leo sometimes came in. He was having a flirtation with Nellie Jacot, whom he undertook to analyze. I had known her intimately for years and resented his appropriation of her. I said some harsh things, but Leo merely laughed at me. Nellie was not taking Leo seriously.

Doing the typing of *The Making of Americans* was a very happy time for me. Gertrude talked over her work of the day, which I typed the following morning. Frequently these were the characters or incidents of the previous day. It was like living history. I hoped it would go on forever.

Our close friend Mildred Aldrich was fearful that *The Mak-*

Gertrude Stein in the Luxembourg Gardens. "She was large and heavy with delicate small hands and a beautifully modeled and unique head. It was often compared to a Roman emperor's. . . ."

—Courtesy of
Erich S. Herrmann, Inc.

Matisse, early in the century. "He . . . wore
gold spectacles, making him look like a German professor."

"Marie Laurencin was in those early days plain. She
had protruding near-sighted eyes, prominent thick lips,
and temperamentally reminded us of some strange
mythological animal."

Gertrude Stein and Alice Toklas in Venice in 1908.

Picasso in the 1930's. When he first met Miss Toklas, he was "very dark with black hair; a lock hanging over one of his marvelous all-seeing brilliant black eyes . . ."

Alice Toklas and Gertrude Stein at home at 27 rue de Fleurus in 1923. As when Miss Toklas first saw the studio, its "walls were covered from *cimaise* to ceiling with pictures." *—Photograph by Man Ray*

—*The Metropolitan Museum of Art, Bequest of Gertrude Stein, 1946*

Two portraits of Gertrude Stein . . .

◀ . . . the 1906 painting by Picasso.

▼ . . . the 1923 statue by Jo Davidson.

—Photo Kollar, Paris

"Rivesaltes, the birthplace of Marshal Joffre, was not far from Perpignan. We drove over to it and I had a photographer take a picture of the house in which the Marshal had been born."

Gertrude Stein and Alice
Toklas in the 1920's. Miss
Stein had learned to drive,
during the war, by "tak-
ing lessons from William
Cook in a Renault taxi he
was driving."

At Bilignin in 1934, where
the summers "were always very busy, enjoyable, and productive."

—*Photographed by Carl Van Vechten*

–Photographs by Bobsy Goodspeed Chapman

In the garden at Bilignin. "Vegetables had become a passion, flowers always had been, my work in the garden was a pleasure."

Basket II with Gertrude Stein at Bilignin. "For years after reading *The Princess Casamassima* I had wanted a white poodle."

Pavel Tchelitchev, with Alice Toklas and Gertrude Stein. "His painting interested Gertrude for a little while. Until it went bad. . . . Then his paintings were moved into the *salon des refusés*."

Bravig Imbs with Alice Toklas and Gertrude Stein in 1928 at Aix-les-Bains. "Bravig Imbs had come over from Dartmouth College where he had written a novel . . ."

Portrait of Gertrude Stein by Carl Van Vechten.

ing of Americans would not give her the pleasure *Three Lives* had. Gertrude had not wanted to discuss anything she was writing. She kept repeating it was for strangers that she wrote. But when the hero died she told Mildred. Mildred was shocked and said, Must you do this? Oh Gertrude, how very sad.

About this time it became my habit to go down evenings from the rue Notre Dame des Champs to the rue de Fleurus. Harriet disapproved of my being alone on the streets at night. However, nothing ever happened until one evening, on the rue Vavin with its narrow sidewalks, unexpectedly a man was standing opposite me. *Eh bien,* said he, do you not intend to give me the right of way? Never, I answered. How difficult the Creoles are, he said as he stepped off the sidewalk. When I told Harriet of this encounter she did not find it humorous. She thought I should be home before midnight.

The first winter at Notre Dame des Champs Miss Blood came up from Florence and told Gertrude she wanted to meet Picasso. Gertrude asked him and some of his friends to come one evening. Miss Blood was going on to a party and she wore a rose-colored dress and her beautiful pearls. Picasso called her the *femme de ménage* of the Princess Murat because she and the Princess Ghika lived at the Gamberaia. She asked him what he considered his contribution to painting. He said, *Je suis le bec Auer,* a gas mantle. Guillaume Apollinaire was as witty as usual, but Miss Blood preferred Picasso's brusque Spanish ways.

There were several parties. The most amusing was the banquet for Henri Rousseau at Picasso's studio. Leo and Gertrude and I met Harriet up at a café in Montmartre near the rue Ravignan, where Marie Laurencin had already arrived and was a little tipsy. She was falling in and out of the arms of

Guillaume Apollinaire, who would put her back on her chair only to find her back in his arms. Then Fernande burst in upon us filled with the tragedy of Félix Potin's not having delivered the dinner she had ordered. I suggested she telephone to remind them, which she did only to find it was too late, nobody answered, the shop was closed.

Fernande said since she had cooked an immense quantity of riz à la Valencienne, which she had learned to prepare in Spain, she would buy accompanying dishes in the quarter. Leo would help Guillaume to get Marie up the hill, Gertrude and Harriet and I would follow. We wended our way up the steep hill to Picasso's atelier, where already many of the guests had arrived. We left our hats and coats in the studio next door of André Salmon.

Fernande had set the dinner table on boards on trestles, which she said was solid if no one leaned too heavily upon it. It was decorated with ivy leaves. Marie Laurencin, her cheek red where Apollinaire had slapped her, was telling us that she would sing some old French songs after dinner. Fernande said the riz à la Valencienne was ready and would be served as soon as Rousseau arrived. When he arrived, Rousseau was given the seat of honor in the center of the table in front of his large portrait of a woman, the purchase of which by Picasso was the reason for the celebration.

The immense dish of rice was indeed excellent. There was a great deal of vin ordinaire consumed. Suddenly there appeared at the door Frédéric and his donkey from his café opposite the studio. Fernande majestically ushered the intruders out saying that they had not been invited and were unwanted. Apollinaire stood on the table to recite his eulogistic poem, and everyone joined in the chorus of *à notre Rousseau*. Rousseau was dazed and beaming. At the end of the poem, Apollinaire jumped off the table. At this point, Salmon disappeared.

Rousseau took his violin out of its case and commenced to play endless dull music. Leo, who was sitting next to him, protected him from the exuberance of the guests. Marie Laurencin sang her songs. Apollinaire asked Harriet and me if we would sing the national song of the Red Indians. He was shocked and unhappy when we told him we did not think that they had one.

When it was quite late we went into Salmon's studio to get our hats and coats. My hat, of which I had been so proud, had been divested of its yellow feather trimming. Salmon had eaten it and a telegram and a box of matches. He seemed unaware of our presence.

We were taking Rousseau home, Gertrude, Leo, Harriet and I. All of us piled into an open fiacre, while Leo sat with the driver. As we were driving down the hill, Salmon came running past us with a wild cry and fled ahead of us in the darkness.

Not long after the banquet to Rousseau, I was walking along the rue de Rennes late in the afternoon. It was quite dark. I suddenly became conscious of footsteps back of me, approaching nearer and nearer. Nothing like this had ever happened to me. Mademoiselle, mademoiselle, the person was saying. Outraged, I turned suddenly to face the voice. It was Rousseau. Mademoiselle, he continued, you should not be out on the streets alone after dark. Permit me to accompany you to wherever you may be going. And we walked to the rue Notre Dame des Champs. I don't think he ever came to see us there but I used to meet him on his occasional appearances at the Saturday evenings at the rue de Fleurus. It was there that he told me one evening that I resembled his wife, dead long ago.

4

I WORKED evenings with Gertrude, staying late at the rue de Fleurus, which Harriet told me worried her. Harriet wanted me to return to the rue Notre Dame des Champs before midnight. I saw that she was lonesome being alone. Finally she told me that she had written to Caroline Helbing to come and spend the winter with us–that is, to sleep at the little hotel near the apartment and have lunch and dinner with us – and that Caroline had accepted and was coming soon.

When she did, I was glad to see her again. I had known her

in San Francisco. She had kept her youthful prettiness. On her return to San Francisco, she was to marry the fiancé to whom she had been engaged for twenty-five years. She laughingly said it would be a silver wedding anniversary when they did marry.

We did not take her to theatres, because she understood little French. But we took her about as much as we could. Afternoons, she and I went to see Paris and to sit at the Café Souflot near the Sorbonne.

Harriet and I had invited Fernande and Marie Laurencin to lunch to meet Caroline. Marie now invited us to come see her flat and meet her mother. Nobody had ever been received in their home. Guillaume Apollinaire had possibly met Marie's mother, but in any case she left the subject of his relation with Marie without comment.

Fernande called for us and she, Gertrude, Caroline, Harriet and I took the metro, which neither Gertrude nor I had the habit of using. At the first station Gertrude said, Come on, we are getting off here, we will take a fiacre. The metro was not to be an experience for us.

Marie lived at the bottom of rue Fontaine. We saw only two rooms of the flat, which looked like a convent, all white with perfect order and no decoration except some of Marie's drawings. Marie had her mother show us the embroideries that she, the mother, had made. They were of monkeys. Marie had a weakness for designs of monkeys. Later, we had a wallpaper that Marie had designed of monkeys on branches of trees, jumping from one branch to another.

Fernande was on her very best behavior, quiet, to please Marie and her mother. Caroline was open-mouthed with wonder and pleasure at the way things were conducted in the little flat. Marie and her mother served very delicate tea. Marie must have gone to a good pâtisserie on the other side of the river.

The history of Marie's mother was strange. Quite young in life she had had an affair with a man who it was rumored was the préfet du Nord. She was from Savoie. When Marie was born, her mother never saw the father again. Nor would she see any man thereafter, so that when she and Marie established themselves in the Paris flat no man was admitted. That would not have been Marie's idea.

The night before Caroline was to leave for America Harriet said to me, We must take Caroline to some restaurant and give her an excellent French meal. So we did, in our quarter. When Harriet commenced to order, I found she was giving Caroline all the dishes that were well known in America – cold salmon, a delicacy in France but not in California, corn on the cob. Poor Caroline was aghast and so she and I ordered another dinner, countermanding Harriet's order.

I took Caroline to the boat train and driving over I said to her, Caroline dear, you must see that when Harriet goes back to America she does not return to Paris because it is already arranged that I should go to stay with Gertrude and Leo at the rue de Fleurus. That is what I suspected, said Caroline, you can count on me. Whereupon Caroline kissed me and I put her on the train.

How she did it I do not know, but Harriet returned to San Francisco with the Mike Steins and soon wrote me that I should close the flat and that the pictures, particularly Matisse's "La Femme aux Yeux Bleus" and the small Harry Phelan Gibb landscape, should be carefully packed and sent to her as she was probably remaining in California. When I told the landlady of Notre Dame des Champs, Madame Vincent Bouguereau, that I was paying for the flat until spring but that the pictures as well as the furniture would be sent to San Francisco now, she put up a vigorous protest and said it was not possible that the flat should be left empty, that I was required by the law to leave the flat furnished. So I consulted an *homme d'affaires* and he said he would see her and make it possible for me to go on with the plan. Which he did.

Leo helped me with the French letters to the lawyer to make certain that I was making it clear to him. And with that I moved over to the rue de Fleurus, where I was given the small room that later we called the *salon des refusés*. There I spent that winter and the following one not too uncomfortably. Mornings I did the typing, and in the afternoon Gertrude and I went out to see friends.

We went to lunch with Mildred Aldrich at a restaurant on the boulevard Montparnasse. And as we were leaving, Mildred spied two men sitting at a table. She wafted her hand towards them saying, Girls come on, I want you to meet my friends. When we got to the table where they were sitting Mildred said, Roger and Henry, this is Alice and Gertrude. She did not know their family names. She called every one by their Christian names, she had gotten the habit from her connection with the theatre. That was the beginning of the acquaintance with Roger Fry and Henry McBride, which lasted many years.

Henry McBride was one of the first of the New York newspapermen, he was really an art critic, who put Gertrude's name prominently forward in connection with pictures and her work. Laugh if you like, he said to her detractors, but laugh with her and not at her.

Gertrude at this time was absorbed in the story of Sylvia Pankhurst, who had been arrested for her too active interest in securing the vote for the women. Miss Pankhurst was told that she must appear at the time her trial would take place. She said, I will be there. She was not. When the trial took place she was somewhere else. She said, That place was where *there* was.

Grace Lounsbery, an early acquaintance of Gertrude from the Johns Hopkins' days, was frequently about at this time. She was an intimate friend of two of Gertrude's intimate friends. Gertrude thought that she was a false alarm.

She was small and not unimpressive in her funny little way. She considered herself a Greek scholar and wrote Greek plays. When she was young, she came to Paris and there fell in with Jean Cocteau. They were the two infant prodigies of the social world. Her plays were produced in a semi-professional manner and she took great satisfaction from this.

Grace Lounsbery amused me but Gertrude found her very tiresome. In those early days she lived in a flat in the rue Boissonade, which was painted in the fashionable manner of the day in black. She considered herself an aesthete and a gourmet. Later she moved, with beautiful Esther Swainson, down to the rue d'Assas in a charming little pavillon. It was Esther who invented the Society for the Encouragement of the Old. She bowed on the street to old gentlemen, which flattered and pleased them.

At Mrs. Eugene Paul Ullman's we had met the Infanta Eulalia of Spain. She had the typical Spanish voice only it was royal, it was not at all raucous, and when she called her lady-in-waiting it was thrilling. She was a half-sister to the Infanta Isabella, whom we met in Palma, but they were as unlike as any half-sisters could be.

Mrs. Ullman brought the Infanta to the rue de Fleurus to see

Gertrude and the pictures. When she was led into the court the Infanta turned on Mrs. Ullman and said, Where are you taking me, what is this place? And she had to be reassured that it was not an ambush.

We met her several times again at Mrs. Ullman's. Several years later, after the war, I was doing errands one day in the rue de la Paix and Gertrude was in the car when I unexpectedly found myself opposite the Infanta. I was a little embarrassed. I did not know what the etiquette was. Should I make myself known or should I let her pass without my doing so? But she gave me no time, she recognized me after four years of war and said, How do you do, Miss Toklas. Where and how is Miss Stein? I said, she was in the car a moment ago and is quite well. I shall be coming to see you, she said.

One evening Leo took Picasso into his studio. When he released him Picasso came in furious saying, He does not leave me alone. It was he who said my drawings were more important than Raphael's. Why can he not leave me alone then with what I am doing now? Leo was quite as disturbed as Picasso and slammed the door between the two rooms. This was the beginning of the trouble between Leo and Gertrude concerning Picasso's painting and her writing. When Leo came in to explain further, she dropped books on the floor to interrupt him.

Gertrude and Leo and I went down to the Casa Ricci in the summer. Gertrude worked and I had conversations with Maddalena, the cook, about Italian cooking and her preparation of it. She had a daughter, Eugenia, to help her and serve at table.

Gertrude had a worn out fountain pen which she had thrown into the scrap basket. Maddalena picked it up and said, Oh, may I have this? Certainly, Gertrude answered, what are you going to do with it? Give it to Eugenia's fiancé, Maddalena explained, he works in the postal service and will be very proud to own a fountain pen.

Gertrude and I took a brief trip to Rome, and there she was tempted to buy a very fine black Renaissance plate that I found through a smart antiquity dealer who had gathered the ancient carpets for Pierpont Morgan. When I asked him if the plate was for sale, he said he would be pleased to have us own it and mentioned the price. Gertrude nodded to me to give me the sign that we would buy it. We had it wrapped very carefully in straw and placed in a wooden box. I carried it back to Fiesole, where we opened it and put it carefully on a high credenza where it could not be disturbed. Gertrude and I both told Maddalena she was not to touch it.

The next morning when Maddalena brought Gertrude's coffee to her bedroom Gertrude was having a bad attack of hiccoughs. Maddalena left the room hurriedly but returned running, crying, Oh signorina, I just let the black plate fall to the floor and it is broken into many pieces. We were very much upset. Maddalena noticing that the hiccoughs had been cured by the fright said, Ah signorina, it was to cure you that I said that, nothing has happened to the plate.

We spent a happy but busy summer, Gertrude writing and seeing some of her Florentine friends. Among them was Mabel Dodge, who had been brought by Mildred Aldrich a year or so before to see Gertrude and Leo in Paris. Mabel Dodge lived in the Villa Curonia at Arcetri where her second husband, Edwin Dodge, an architect, had very elaborately made over the enormous living room.

Mabel's little son by her first husband said he wanted to fly and stood on the balustrade of the terrace stretching out his arms. Mabel encouraged him, saying, Fly my dear, fly if you want to. But the boy did not, he stepped down. Edwin said to Mabel, There is nothing like a Spartan mother.

One day Mabel asked me to go to the railroad station to meet Constance Fletcher, who was coming from her home in Venice. You will know her, said Mabel, because she is deaf and will be wearing a purple robe. When I got to the railroad station Miss Fletcher came up to me. She was wearing not a purple robe but a bright green one, she was not deaf but nearly blind and peered through her lorgnons.

When we went back to Paris after the summer, we returned to the rue de Fleurus. We passed a hardworking winter. Gertrude worked until the birds commenced to twitter before she turned out the lights in the studio and went upstairs to bed.

Picasso and Fernande had by this time separated definitively. Shortly before the separation Picasso and Fernande and Fernande's new friend Eve came to see us one evening. They brought with them the painter Marcoussis, with whom Eve had been living. Gertrude said to me after they left, Is Picasso leaving Fernande for this young thing? He was. They were very happy in the beginning.

Picasso had left Montmartre, never to live there again, and after a succession of places had found a pavillon on the boulevard Raspail. Everyone was moving to Montparnasse from various parts of Paris, it had become the center of the modern painters. It was at the pavillon one evening that Guillaume Apollinaire said of the brooch Gertrude was wearing, a large dark coral set in a large piece of green malachite, A fried egg but more unctuous. Later that evening Guillaume said something to which I answered him wittily but which I do not remember. Picasso said to me, You can only get the better of Guillaume when he is a little tipsy.

From the boulevard Raspail, Picasso and Eve moved to an apartment in the rue Schoelcher overlooking the cemetery of Montparnasse. When we went to see them, Eve would have a cup of chocolate brought to her and sip it. Pablo was offended by her lack of hospitality.

Eve was in frail health later, and went to a nursing home where she died.

The following summer when Leo decided to go to Settignano and take the little house on the property of the Gamberaia that Miss Blood proposed, it was on the condition that he come there unmarried. He had been going with a girl of the Quarter, Nina, but he had not yet married her. We wondered what Miss Blood would say, because Leo went down to the little house with Nina. Miss Blood apparently accepted this situation for the moment.

Gertrude and I decided not to rent the Casa Ricci but to go to Spain. Mildred Aldrich came to see us off at the train. She was almost as excited as we were, though Gertrude had already been to Spain with Leo in 1903.

We stopped first in Burgos. The beautiful Gothic cathedral there was my first introduction to Spaniards and things Spanish. Outside the cathedral was a group of children who were becoming an annoyance. One little girl was preparing to go into the cathedral with us, having put on her head a little veil. She had green eyes and asked me for some money. I pretended not to hear her. In the cathedral she followed us about and said, A penny, kind sir? We finally got out of the cathedral by a side door without her seeing us. Her green eyes and her ways suggested Becky Sharp.

In Valladolid I saw, at one of the altars of the cathedral, two beaten and painted ornaments with arabesque designs to imitate artificial flowers. I was so enchanted with these that I asked the sexton if he could give me the address of the descendants of the man who had made them. I thought they might still have in their workshop some or something like them. I finally found two ornaments like those in the cathedral but unpainted, which I bought for a small sum and which are now on the dining-room chimney piece of the rue Christine.

On the way south we stopped at Ávila. We saw from the train the town in the distance with its old wall and cathedral. Gertrude said to me, This is the town where St. Therese was born. St. Therese became the inspiration for *Four Saints in Three Acts.*

At the station there was a coach with four mules, with bells on their harness, waiting to take us to the inn. It was a noisy rough trip over the cobbled roads of Ávila, but when we got there we were delighted to find the inn clean and orderly. They had put our things in the hallway, they said the rooms would have to be scrubbed before we could go into them. When one of the rooms was drying with the windows open, I heard a mechanical piano playing on the road below. It was a wedding party that was having a supper in the dining room. I liked the music. I threw small change to keep them there.

I said to Gertrude, I am not going to leave here, I am staying, and Gertrude said, What do you mean? I said, I am enraptured with Ávila and I propose staying. Gertrude said, Well, I will stay two weeks instead of two days, but I could not work here, you know that. It quieted me temporarily.

We walked around the town after an excellent dinner. Spanish cooking in Ávila was better than in most towns. In the morning we walked to St. Therese's church and to a chapel completely covered in beaten gold with coral ornaments sent in the seventeenth century from America. I located a pastry shop that still remains unexcelled. We got back in time for lunch. At the lunch table there was a colonel of the quartermaster corps who said he could supply me with a horse for riding. Everybody was doing things for us. We walked way out into the country where a colonel of the civil guard sent two of his men to accompany us so that we would not be annoyed by the population.

We were fortunate to be in Ávila at this time, for a Mass was to be said for a visiting bishop who was to be received after the Mass at lunch by the bishop of Ávila.

At the pastry shop we saw the dishes prepared for the lunch. Foods of all kinds fantastically decorated with vegetables, salads arranged to represent the cathedral, pieces mounted in caramel and meringue. The ices they dared not show us, fearing they would melt.

The effect in the vast cathedral of the singing with full orchestra was magnificent. The priests were wearing vestments embroidered in China in the sixteenth century. That afternoon we were shown these vestments and many others.

Finally we had to leave Ávila, having ordered a lunch at the pastry shop to eat on the train taking us to Madrid, which was no less beautiful and quite as exciting as the three northern towns we had seen. In Madrid we went frequently to the Prado, spending long mornings looking at the Goyas, Velázquez's, and Grecos.

On the street one morning we ran into Pichot and he said, What can I do for you here in Spain? I said, Is there any good dancing? Oh, he said, marvelous, you are just in time for the greatest dancer Spain has seen in years, La Argentina. He told us where to find her and the hours she danced and I said, What about bullfights? Oh, he said, the great bullfighters will be here next week. So we had everything prepared for us.

The Argentina danced in a little music hall holding not more than three hundred people. Her performance was after a mixed programme which we sat through to have good seats for her performance, as none were reserved. I remember that the first night there was an American bicycle rider who performed cleverly. The Argentina was a woman then in her late twenties or early thirties, plain but with great appeal. She wore the classic Spanish dancer's costume of the full fairly long skirt trimmed with chenille balls, sleeves to the elbows, the bodice cut in a modest V, a large tortoise-shell comb in her hair. With her famous smile, she danced the classic dance of Spain in which she did not move more than a few feet from the center of the stage. The audience was silent, spellbound, and went off its head when the dance was over. This was a performance that had commenced at eight o'clock in the evening. There was another performance at midnight. Gertrude proposed that we should go back to the hotel and return to the music hall for the Argentina's last performance.

When we got back to the music hall we discovered that we were the only women in the audience. We were uncertain what might happen. But nothing happened, the audience was enthralled as we were by her witchery. They clapped a good deal to the time of her step. It was more exciting than the Russian ballet.

The bullfight was the first one I had ever seen. Gertrude had been to a bullfight when she had been in Spain with Leo. I had a black costume made in the fashion of Spain that I called my

Spanish disguise, so that I remained unnoticed. It consisted of a black feather hat, a black satin coat, black fan and gloves.

We had gotten seats that morning at the box office where the subscribers came to pick up their tickets and I said to the man, We have no tickets reserved but I must have the very best in the first row in the shade under the President's box. And he said, Yes yes, and gave me two tickets which I had to trust were what I had asked for. In the afternoon they turned out to be so.

Gertrude would say, Do not look, when a horse was being gored. She would say, Now you can look, when the horse had been led away.

There was at a café a singer, Preciosilla, of astonishing beauty and brilliance. Her enormous diamond earrings were no brighter than her eyes. Later I was able to buy the music of one of her songs and when I told Picasso the words of its chorus he said, Fortunately you do not know enough Spanish to understand it. Later Gertrude wrote a portrait of her.

Our hotel was on the calle San Geronimo. When we came in late, the night watchman with his lantern opened the door for us with a very large key. In the hotel, on the floor, the concierge was rolled up in a blanket asleep, and we had to walk over him to get to the stairs to go to our rooms.

Near the hotel were two or three captivating antique shops, where we bought an endless quantity of objects as gifts and for ourselves. Amongst them was an apothecary pot, for which I had a wooden box with a handle made to carry it back to France. Our hand luggage became bulkier at every purchase.

When the Argentina's season was over we decided to go on to Toledo. At the hotel in Madrid when I spoke of going to Toledo they said, It is a small town, you can see it in one day.

But we left Madrid to stay in Toledo where there were Grecos, a fine cathedral and many churches.

The Corpus Christi procession at Toledo was under an awning stretched over a narrow street. Those in the procession carried long large lighted candles so that the mixture of daylight and artificial light was a curious one. We had secured seats through the hotel on a balcony under the awning. The balconies all along the route were draped in fine old tapestries. All about the street were people hurrying to find their place either to watch or to take part in the procession. Little children holding candles were singing canticles while they waited to be told where to fall in line.

In the hotel in Gertrude's room the table was a little unsteady, and Gertrude evened the one leg that was short by placing pennies under it. She was writing every morning and she said to me, Perhaps you had better take the pennies and put them aside for tomorrow. I said, Oh no, no one will touch them. If they do, they will put them right back again. Which they did.

From Toledo we went to the Escorial, its somber landscape and architecture the most impressive in Spain. "The Conversion of Saint Maurice" in the picture gallery was one of the finest large Grecos I saw. The first impression of its overwhelming beauty has not grown dimmer in fifty years.

Then we proceeded to Cuenca, which Harry Phelan Gibb had recommended. We got there late, when it was already dark, and had a copious dinner of wild game. Gertrude said that she would have to have the windows closed in both the rooms because she feared the sudden and deep descent into the wild torrent in the valley below. As she could not bear heights, I agreed and slept fitfully without air. The next morning we looked out and found that the windows gave on a mountain. The torrent was on the other side of the hotel.

I said to the maid when she brought breakfast trays, I want two pitchers of boiling water. She brought me one and I said, But I asked for two. Oh, said the maid, I did not know strangers needed hot water, I thought it was only Spaniards who bathed.

On the walks in the country the charming quiet children would come up and touch my dress and say to each other, It is not silk. It was not, it was Dutch batik cotton. One little girl asked me how was it that I had fresh flowers on my hat at an hour before the train could bring them from Madrid. I said, Feel them, they are of silk and velvet, they are not fresh but artificial. The young girls came up one by one to touch them.

On the walk up the pleasant little valley, with its small homes and small cultivated gardens, we were joined by civil guards as we had been in Ávila. We were once more being protected by the governor of the province.

From Cuenca we went to Córdova. The cathedral had not been restored as it is today. Córdova was hot. At night I could not sleep. Gertrude gave me a basin of cold water and my bath sponge and all night I sprinkled water over my body. The cathedral of Córdova seemed more Arab – that is, more Mohammedan – than Christian.

From Córdova we went to Seville, where it was very hot and where I ate innumerable ices during the day, which disturbed Gertrude's stomach. We stayed at the hotel that Matisse had recommended which was comfortable and where the food was excellent.

The cathedral in Seville was a treasure house. The high wrought-iron grilles, before the chapels, had faded cardinals' hats on the top of them. The high altar was closed by a high iron grille except when Mass was being said, then its door was opened. The music was movingly beautiful. One day Mass was being said at an altar before which we happened to be standing when suddenly a bishop who was officiating came down the steps before the altar. Gertrude and I flew to one side to give the bishop room to pass.

In Seville there was a long narrow street where the members of various clubs sat at tables on sidewalks and on the street. Some forty years later, when I went back to Seville for the first time, I was able to locate a bookshop on that street.

Down by the river gypsies gathered, not at all welcoming the two strangers we were.

Gertrude had a serious attack of colitis. I was frightened and took her hurriedly to Gibraltar, where she happily recovered. We took a small boat across to Tangier and stayed at a hotel that Matisse and Madame Matisse had stayed at, which was amusing and quite comfortable.

At that time it was not possible to enter Fez, because there had been warlike activities. We had not any intention of going to Fez but wanted to walk about Tangier. We found a Mohammedan whose name was Mohammed, and he took us where it was safe to go. Mohammed was an adopted son of the sultan of Tangier, who had many adopted children. He had had a European education and spoke French fluently, and even some English. When we were about to leave and said good-bye he said, Next year, when you come, there will be a tramway on the coast here and that will be nice. He told us the date when the sultan was going to abdicate and how much money he would receive from the French authorities to do so. The date happened to be my brother's birthday so I remembered it. One day I was surprised to find in the newspaper that the sultan had abdicated and for the sum that Mohammed had said. Later, when we were at Palma de Mallorca, we told this story to the French consul there, Monsieur Marchand, who had been liaison officer between Marshal Lyautey and the Arabs. If you had only told us. Fancy your knowing what we wanted and needed to know, he moaned.

On the return from Tangier we went to Ronda, a little town that I called Elizabethan because of the architecture of the small houses. On one of our walks, Gertrude took me to a little river and commenced jumping from one stone to another to cross it. She said to me, Come on, why do you hesitate? I said it was because the stones were not stepping stones but skipping stones. However, I did finally get across.

We stayed there for several days and went on to Granada, which Gertrude had known but which I had never seen. It was the month of August, and there was a full harvest moon. The English consul there, seeing us wandering about, took us on long walks over the roofs of some of the houses.

We fell madly in love with Granada. There were the gypsies who danced and walked beautifully with their wide skirts and swinging step. It was there that Gertrude commenced to write the portraits of the gypsies.

Finally, reluctantly, we returned to France. But not to stay, for in the autumn of that year we visited Mabel Dodge at the Villa Curonia.

It was then that Gertrude wrote the *Portrait of Mabel Dodge*. Constance Fletcher was fascinated with the portrait and said to Mabel, We must have this printed at once, I will do the correction of proof, it will not take any time to have it printed. Mabel then proposed to bind the little booklets in modern prints from old Florentine woodcuts. Constance wanted to correct the spelling of the words honor and sailor with an ou in the English manner, though she was American born and bred.

Constance's mother had run away with her and her young brother's tutor from Newburyport, Massachusetts. They had gone to Florence, where the tutor became a painter. Later they spent a winter in Cairo, where Constance wrote her first novel when she was eighteen. One of her novels, *Kismet,* was a best seller before there were best sellers. After its publication Constance settled in London for a short while and wrote a play, *The Canary,* which was also a great success. There she met and became engaged to Lord Lovelace, a descendant of Byron, but he gradually cooled so they never married. After this she came to settle in Venice, where she lived to very nearly the end of her life. I learned later that her family was Swiss and that she had gone to Switzerland from Venice and died there.

The painter Haweis and his wife, later Mina Loy, were living in Florence at that time. Mina was beautiful, intelligent, sympathetic and gay. We joined them for lunch, where a friendship with her commenced that lasted over the years.

One day Mina deserted Haweis and their little son, and ran away to Mexico to meet Craven, a nephew of Mrs. Oscar Wilde. Craven was a very handsome Englishman who wrote a pamphlet on the salon paintings that caused a scandal and who boxed for pleasure. He mysteriously disappeared off the coast of Mexico fleeing the English conscription when war was declared by the English in 1914. Mina always insisted that he had been drowned, but there was no proof of that.

Mabel had met and invited André Gide for dinner at the villa. When the dinner hour was approaching, Mabel sent word to me saying, If you are dressed, go down at once. If not, hurry and do so to receive André Gide who is due now. Which I did, making conversation with him until Mabel appeared. After dinner Mabel, stretched out on one of the long sofas, was talking in a low voice to Monsieur Gide who, sitting opposite, was leaning over her. Mina thought this highly ridiculous and danced about with an imaginary partner. This did not disturb Mabel. Nor did it disturb Monsieur Gide, who could not see Mina's antics.

5

—

W<small>E HAD</small> been advised by Mira Edgerly to go to London and see the publishers about the publication of Gertrude's work. She had said to write in advance, giving some account of Gertrude's position in the art world, which I did not think had anything to do with the publication of her work. Mira also said that she would ask her friends, Colonel Rogers and Mrs. Rogers, to expect us with her for a weekend at River Hill in Kent.

Mira was an extraordinarily beautiful Californian, though

she had not been born there. She had had in England an exceptional social and artistic success as a miniaturist, and had painted many portraits of the royal family. She was in a position to do anything she pleased in England.

At the coronation of the King one of the peeresses was suddenly taken ill and Mira replaced her, the official dress for the occasion being of the right size. Mira was tall and stately. She used to take a string and stretch it under her nose, making it sharper and less beautiful, saying she was Kathryn Kidder, the great Shakespearian actress.

Mira recommended a small hotel not far from the National Gallery, where we stopped and where she called for us to go down to River Hill. At the station at River Hill there was a carriage to meet us. None of that world were indulging in automobiles.

Mrs. Rogers had a delicate beauty. When she took us herself to the rooms we were to occupy I saw a beautiful Chinese porcelain and said, Oh how beautiful, how did you come to have it, because it is a museum piece. That I know nothing about, Mrs. Rogers replied, it was here when I came.

The children, numerous, were all extremely lovely. One little girl attached herself to Gertrude and we could not separate her from Gertrude, she was like sticky candy.

There were people for lunch and for dinner. We walked quite a distance to get to the dining room. They had two dining rooms, as a matter of fact. The small one only held twelve. There were no men servants indoors, there were only maids, very tall and rustling in starched clothes and caps. Gertrude said they looked like archangels.

Colonel Rogers took us driving in the country. The gardens at River Hill, which were very large, were nothing compared to those at Knole, where we were taken through the house to see rooms that had been furnished for a visit by Queen Elizabeth the First. The furnishings remained intact. I particularly remember a very large silver-framed mirror. Then we were taken to a room where you could see the roofs of several wings of the house, all very steep. There was a tale of some member of the family hiding on the roof, I do not know from what.

The next morning Colonel Rogers took us to a meeting of the hunt, which he had to forego because of us but where we met the master of the hunt, the ex-Viceroy of India, Lord Hastings.

Mira had an appointment in London and left that afternoon. We went back to London the next day and commenced our rounds of the editors to whom I had written from Paris. They were all extremely affable but could make nothing of Gertrude's literature. They thanked me for sending it to them, but no publication was suggested. Only one of them, John Lane of The Bodley Head, was encouraging.

Roger Fry, who had visited the rue de Fleurus, asked us to spend a day with him in the country. He was a Quaker and a descendant of chocolate manufacturers and had inherited considerable wealth. He could afford to buy pictures and establish an art center in London. He had discovered Picasso for himself.

It was Roger Fry who had brought Clive Bell and Mrs. Bell to see Gertrude Stein in Paris. Mrs. Bell was the very plain sister of the very beautiful Virginia Woolf. They were daughters of Sir Leslie Stephen. The two sisters, impersonating Indian princesses, had once been received by an admiral on a man-of-war and cannon had been fired in their honor. A typical English prank.

Clive Bell was in those days witty and amusing, before he became pretentious. He said that when he traveled with Roger Fry and his wife they always wanted only to see first-rate works of art, he only cared for second-rate ones.

The Clive Bells' two little children were very lovely and looked like cherubs, not at all like their parents. The boy was killed in the Spanish revolution and the girl is now Mrs. Edward Garnett.

We went back to Paris but returned to London the following year, after the assassination of the Archduke, not suspecting that war was inevitable. This time we came to see John Lane, who in the meantime had come to see Gertrude in Paris. Mrs. John Lane was an American. Her husband said that he relied a great deal upon her judgment and had given a copy of *Three Lives* to her to read. Would we come to his home on the following Sunday when they would be receiving?

So putting on our best bibs and tuckers we went on Sunday. Mildred Aldrich had said that John Lane was an eagle or a serpent, she did not know which, but in any case he would defend you. It was he who had discovered Aubrey Beardsley and published *The Yellow Book*.

When we got to their home in Park Lane their drawing rooms were filled with people. Mrs. Lane looked like my old piano teacher, a French woman, from San Francisco. Whether she had French blood or not I never knew. She told Gertrude at once, I will advise my husband to take the book and publish it, it will have a success in England. Which was so different from the publishers of the year before.

The subject of conversation was war. One of the editors of the London *Times* was there and I remember him saying, I shall not be able to eat figs in Provence this year.

We had accepted an invitation from Hope Mirrlees' mother to visit her at Cambridge. We also received an invitation to stay with Logan Pearsall Smith, but mobilization prevented us from taking a train. The trains were being requisitioned for the movement of troops.

The Mirrlees were giving dinner parties for Gertrude and at one of them I sat next to A.E. Housman. He said to me, Since you are from California, tell me about your great ichthyologist, Dr. David Starr Jordan. Oh, I said, he was a friend of my grandfather. So I told him all I knew about the president of Leland Stanford University.

At the Mirrlees' one night we met Dr. Alfred North Whitehead and Mrs. Whitehead. After dinner he asked me if he could take me to the garden where we would have coffee. I did not know who he was at the time, and only when I saw his face under a lamp did I recognize him. He had a most benign sweet smile and a simplicity that comes only in geniuses. He was my third genius for whom the bell rang. The first two had been Gertrude Stein and Picasso.

We dined with the Whiteheads again in London, and Mrs. Whitehead then asked us to visit them at their country home in Lockridge the following weekend. Little did we know that the weekend would extend well into the next month. Louise Hayden later said, You were asked for a weekend and you stayed six weeks.

When war was declared, Dr. Whitehead read aloud the frightening news from the newspapers. But he kept his quiet serenity.

Bertrand Russell came to visit the Whiteheads and held forth on pacifism. Mrs. Whitehead as hostess could say nothing, but

Gertrude – who had known Russell on a visit to England with Leo – spoke very harshly to him.

The Whiteheads had a very young son and an older one, who was in the country recuperating from an illness, and a young daughter. Mrs. Whitehead was worried about North, the older son. She was worried lest he try to enlist, so she telegraphed him to come home at once. He had, in fact, tried to enlist. She felt that he should have a commission and go off at once as an officer, so she went immediately to London where she saw Kitchener. Kitchener had once been an intimate friend of her husband's brother, a bishop of the Church of England in India. Mrs. Whitehead came back with a commission for North.

We proposed going to London to retrieve our trunks and to draw money on our letters of credit, and Mrs. Whitehead came with us. She wished to see if she could do anything to help the Belgians. At the junction we were surprised to see Lady Astley, whom we had met through Mira Edgerly in Paris. She had come to say good-bye to her son, who was in the Guards. They had been ordered to France. That was the first we knew that England was sending troops to France.

In London the station was crowded with young men who were leaving school to go off to the war.

We hastened back to the country. The war news became alarming. Gertrude refused to get up, preferring to stay in bed with her eyes closed but not asleep. When the Germans were finally stopped at the Marne, I hurried up to Gertrude's room to tell her. She would not believe me. Are you sure? she said. Yes, I said. Sure and certain. You do not need to worry for the moment, at least.

The Battle of the Marne so completely eased our minds that

the future was not as terrifying as it had been. A wire came from Nellie Jacot saying, *Tout va bien nullement de danger t'embrasse Nellie*. This we showed to everybody at the Whiteheads'. They did not think it as ridiculous as we did but took it as a sign of great encouragement.

Amongst the people at the Whiteheads' was Lytton Strachey, a near neighbor. We had met him the year before at Ethel Sands', the day we met George Moore. His delicate squeaky voice was more penetrating during those early war days than it had been before. His sister was in Germany and he was worried about getting her out. Evelyn Whitehead said to him, You should appeal to the British ambassador in Germany. Lytton Strachey said, But how can I? I have never met him.

At last we went up to London to get our papers from the Embassy, to cross the Channel. In the offices of the Embassy they were talking all languages but a great deal of German, which horrified us.

A secretary at the Embassy said to us, What can I do for you? Give us a temporary passport to go back to our home in Paris, Gertrude said. Oh, I cannot do that, he replied. But you have done it, said Gertrude. Oh no, said he, not possibly. Gertrude then said, I had not intended to use my friend's name, but look up the name of Mildred Aldrich and you will see that papers were given to her. He disappeared and came back a little while after and said quite humbly, You are right. And he gave us our papers.

He said, Will you stand up please and swear loyalty to your country. I said enthusiastically, Oh I would love to. And he said Yes, in a businesslike way.

I went to the hotel to get our trunks and repack them. So

hastily was this done that I lost a lovely old Wedgwood plate, having fatally packed it under a heavy malachite bowl.

When I think of it now I wonder that we were able to take our enormous Innovation trunk into France.

On the Channel boat there were many very sad Belgian officers who had escaped from Belgium and were now entering France. Their eyes were watchful but tired. It was our first experience with the eyes of soldiers.

The train trip was a strange one. We zigzagged around the country to avoid the French army and only got into Paris when it was dark.

Paris was all but deserted just then. Mildred Aldrich forced by economy had closed her Paris flat, given her canaries away and moved her furniture and books to Huiry, a hilltop hamlet on the Marne, where she had just settled when war was declared. We went to visit her, and she told us of the Battle of the Marne.

Conscription had taken so many of our French friends. Derain and Braque were off at once. Picasso as a Spaniard was of course not conscripted and said good-bye to them then. Later he said, That was the last time I saw them because when they returned they were not the friends to whom I had said good-bye.

Herbin, a small painter, small in every sense, was released from the army because he was not strong enough to carry a knapsack. He was befriended by Roger Fry and stayed with him some time in London. Henri Marchand came back from the Levant and was mobilized. Delaunay was in Spain and mysteriously escaped conscription there. Matisse was mobilized as a guardian of the railroad bridges. Because of his feeble eyesight he was not taken as an active soldier.

Guillaume Apollinaire had never taken out French nationality. He had been born in Italy of a Polish mother and an Italian father and had gone to school in southern France. When war was declared, he volunteered in the French army as an artillery officer. After falling off his horse several times, he was sent to the front where during the early part of the war he received a head wound and was trepanned. Gertrude and I saw him briefly one afternoon in Paris in '17 at a tea party at Chanel's in the garden of her home in the Faubourg Saint-Honoré. His head was bandaged and he looked handsomer than ever.

In the spring of 1915 we went down to Palma de Mallorca. We had been there two summers before and had liked it. We traveled by train to Barcelona and by boat across the Mediterranean to Palma. We were told we were being chased by a German submarine, but we got safely to Palma in the early morning.

We went to a pension that had been recommended by some English people but which we found not satisfactory. When we were about to leave, William Cook found us. He had been on the boat with Jeanne, his Bretonne friend. He wanted to know what he could do to help us. I said we were moving to the Hotel Mediterráneo and I would leave Gertrude with the luggage as hostage while I looked at the new rooms in the hotel. The hotel promised well. Cook and I returned at once and got Gertrude out of pawn.

We finally settled at a branch of the Mediterráneo that was on the sea overlooking the harbor of Palma and the cathedral. Cook and Jeanne took us on long walks up to Genova and into the olive groves. The cathedral square with the archbishop's palace at Fenaluch enchanted us. Cook also took us to a bull-fight at Inca, where Jeanne saw her first bull being killed. She could only think of the worth on the market for an animal of that size.

Waiting for the train at the little station of Inca to take us back to Palma, Cook in conversation with a native was offered a drink of aqua vitae and knowing how to drink without touching his lips to the bottle he said, The ladies will taste this also. But I spilled mine over my chin and Gertrude refused to take any.

At the station there was a shrine, a little grotto of the Virgin, that touched me. As we left the little town, all the windmills were in action. Jeanne said, looking out of the window of the train as the evening commenced, This is the hour when the poet works.

Then we rented a furnished house at Terreno, just outside of Palma, from a retired major of the army. He came with his oldest daughter to take an inventory, but she told us she could no longer write. How did that happen? I asked. Did you never learn? Oh, she said, I learned how to write at the convent but as I have had no occasion to write since then I have forgotten how.

We bought a Mallorcan hound, reddish brown with black stripes across the body, and had a hard time training him, he was not housebroken. When we went to Barcelona for the dentist we would bring back dozens of tuberoses from the flower market on the Ramblas. Gertrude told me to train Polybe to smell them, not to eat them as he had been doing. I told him, but he was not obedient and went on trying to eat them. Gertrude said, Whisper it to him. But that was not effective either.

As the summer was very hot we left the windows and doors open during the night and he jumped over the iron gate and escaped. One night we went for a walk with Cook and Jeanne up to Genova and there in the moonlight Polybe and several comrades of his were dancing in a circle on the hilltop. I had never before seen dogs dance in a circle in the moonlight and was fascinated with their performance.

Later Cook told me that we were not training Polybe well. He was chasing, so Cook said, the goats and few sheep about Palma and the peasants said they would kill the animal if they caught him. So we took to tying him up, the poor dog, and he barked and cried so that the next-door neighbor threw a note onto our terrace saying, If your dog does not stop his noise I will kill him. We had to protect Polybe against the ferocity of the Mallorcans who, like Arabs, did not like dogs.

From Palma we went on a little boat to Valencia, asking Cook to come as our guest for the week's fiesta of peasant dancing and great bullfighters. There we saw Gallito and Gallo, his older brother, in some remarkable feats in the bull ring. I had got as usual good seats in the shade under the President's box for the three of us. The King and the Queen came to the bullfights and she turned her eyes away from the ring. On her wedding day, she had had a bad experience. A bomb was thrown into their carriage in an attempt to kill the King, some of the blood from the slight wound the King received staining her white wedding dress.

The peasant dancing was interesting though not professional. Much of the dancing was traditional and the audience clapped the beat of the time.

When we got back to Palma we found that Jeanne and our Bretonne cook had gotten to know each other and gone on a walk carrying a hot gigot, which our cook had baked. This intimacy made the situation a bit difficult.

When we had to go to Barcelona for the dentist or to get warm winter clothes as the season progressed, we found that the *cocottes* were astonishingly good looking and well dressed, carrying themselves with dignity. There was nothing like them in France. Our dentist was apparently the only American dentist in Spain, he was the dentist of the King. He told us that the King had said it was the *canaille* and himself who were for the allies, nearly everybody else was for the Germans.

We prepared now to leave Palma and return to Paris. When we went to the American consul to have our passports visaed he refused to do so saying, How do I know they are legal? Have the French consul visa them first. It was embarrassing for us to have to admit our consul's inefficiency. We went to the French consulate. Oh, said the consul, that is all right. If you don't remember me, I remember you. You were in Madrid in 1912 and 1913, I cashed your cheques at the Crédit Lyonnais. As I am too old to be mobilized, I have been loaned to the consulate. Armed with his visa we returned to our consul who, unashamed, signed them. Take care, he said, that a German spy does not steal them. You had better sleep on them under your pillows.

Gertrude, never having enough to read, had subscribed to Mudie's circulating library in London. It was now my pleasant duty to make out the list of books and pack those that were being returned. Gertrude had a very catholic taste in reading but she particularly liked the out-of-print copies of English officers' autobiographies, which caused a contretemps in Spain.

On the little coasting steamer that we took from Palma we stopped at Cartagena, where the prisoners from the Spanish war in Africa were being held. We saw their families hanging around the prison to have a moment's conversation with the men. As we got off the boat to go to Granada by train, we were held up by the Spanish police from Cartagena who wanted to know what we were doing. They were rather rough. They pointed to the canvas bag which held the Mudie books. Taking one out a police officer pointed to the illustrations of maps and said, What are you doing with these? I said, She reads them because they are the history of English officers. What has that to do with you? he asked. I said, It is history. Whereupon he called the captain. I thought the conversation had gone far enough and asked the captain to explain to the police officer that we were innocent travelers and that these were history books. Which the captain did. The explanation was accepted and we were free to take the train.

We returned to a disturbed France.

6

WE decided that we would at once have to busy ourselves with some war work. As we were walking down the rue des Pyramides I suddenly saw a Ford car driven by a young American woman in uniform stop opposite to where we were standing. I said to Gertrude, Wait a minute, I am going in to inquire about this. I was taken to the chairman of the American Fund for French Wounded, Mrs. Isabel Lathrop, a good-looking gentlewoman dressed in a pink garden party hat and dress with a string of pearls. In spite of her frivolous appearance, she had great instinct for work and for the efficient management of her society.

She listened to my question and said, Yes, you can work for us but you must provide a Ford truck to deliver supplies at the hospitals, as all of our trucks are used by the people who brought them over. But if you can take charge of the classification of what is going out to hospitals, come at once and do that while you wait for the truck.

Gertrude wrote to her cousin, Fred Stein, for the truck she wanted him to send. I went to work. The supplies kept flowing in and out and everybody was busy. William Gwin, whom I had known as a little boy in San Francisco, and who had volunteered with the Serbian army and been discharged after he was wounded in the Serbian retreat, was working opening cases and making out hospital lists. He was helped by an old ex-admiral, who more slowly did the same work.

Finally, early in 1917, the Ford from Fred Stein arrived. Gertrude had been practicing her driving in those hot summer afternoons, taking lessons from William Cook in a Renault taxi he was driving. Now she drove the Ford, on which we sat on packing cases, out to a nearby workshop to have the body made.

At last we were notified to come out and take possession of the converted truck. Driving into Paris, Gertrude got stuck between two streetcars coming in opposite directions and had to be pushed off the track. The next morning I gave Gertrude no time to reflect. We went over to the rue des Pyramides to report to Mrs. Lathrop that we were ready to go to work.

We were given a list of supplies we were to carry to a hospital at Saint Cloud, our first delivery. There we were naturally well received. I got the proper papers signed and the next morning we took them over to Mrs. Lathrop, who then asked us where we would like to open a depot. I said Perpignan because we knew some people there.

We started off one cold snowy morning, armed with a Michelin guide and innumerable maps. We spent the first night at Saulieu, where the proprietor of the hotel gave me an unpleasant feeling that he was German. But he was only wearing German clothes he had brought from Potsdam, where he had been the Emperor's chef. He made a plain but delicious supper for us.

The next morning we were on our way again. At Arnay-le-Duc going down a steep hill in the snow we were stopped by a procession of ducks crossing the road. Gertrude's skill in driving did not include the unexpected.

When we got to Perpignan, we settled in a small, quiet, friendly little hotel. The landlady said I might use a large empty room on the first floor near the entrance. The cases from our society had already arrived at the station, and Gertrude had her first experience of loading into the truck as many cases as it would hold. We kept returning for more until all of them had been delivered at the hotel. Then I devised means of sorting the supplies without having them seen by any of the doctors or nurses. I had, for example, a case of five hundred thermometers. It would not do to have those seen. Everybody would want one, whether they needed it then or were merely keeping it for future use. So the cases were opened, examined, and placed on the floor, one piled on top of another in a manner that made steps I could climb.

I learned my way with some difficulty until finally I was a professional worker.

In Perpignan there were a great many hospitals of all sizes,

some of which were used for the evacuated wounded and
tubercular Serbian soldiers who had gone through the retreat.
The soldiers were pitiable, gentle, sad.

Jo Davidson's wife had opened, with the aid of American
friends, a hospital for wounded officers, and we saw her and
her mother frequently. She told me to pay no attention to the
director of the military hospital at Perpignan, who would ask
for supplies which he would not give away but would keep for
himself. I said he had already told me he needed silk pajamas.

The Willie Dunbar Jewetts lived near Perpignan in a Mallorcan fortified castle, which he had bought after having seen
the advertisement of it in an architects' review. They were living with Mrs. Jewett's mother, Mrs. Prendergast. He was from
San Francisco and she, Mrs. Jewett, from New Orleans. Her
mother, a rabid Southerner, was of French descent and believed in the French Catholic cause as expressed by the Action
Française. She amused me but Gertrude found her a bore.

With the Willie Dunbar Jewetts we visited a hospital they
had been generously aiding. Then we spent the night in their
castle. It had an oubliette from which Willie Dunbar Jewett
had fished up with a rope and a hook on the end of it endless
ancient objects – iron andirons, candlesticks, but no furniture.
The furniture had rotted, if ever there had been any there. He
gave us a pair of iron andirons which we later took back to
Paris, finally giving them to Janet Scudder for the home that
she had built.

Mrs. Jewett was practical and tireless. Willie Jewett was less
practical. He had once gone to Spain and driven back a pair
of royal mules in their silver harness, which he drove around
the country to the delight of the natives.

While waiting for more supplies I was shocked to receive a

letter from our society in Paris, which told me what would be coming to us but was signed Mrs. Francis Shaw, chairman. Mrs. Shaw was a handsome Swiss member of our committee whom I had met in Paris. What has become, I said to Gertrude, of Mrs. Lathrop? This is frightening. But nothing had happened. It was just a moment's aberration of Mrs. Shaw. Mrs. Lathrop remained our chairman.

Rivesaltes, the birthplace of Marshal Joffre, was not far from Perpignan. We drove over to it and I had a photographer take a picture of the house in which the Marshal had been born. From this photograph I had a thousand postcards printed to sell in the United States for the benefit of our society, which pleased Mrs. Lathrop in Paris and produced additional funds.

When our work at Perpignan was over, we returned to Paris. On the way up I gave Gertrude a half cold chicken to eat in one hand while she was driving, so as not to waste any time. On the road someone told us that the American army was coming into Nevers that evening. Before we got there we passed stray Americans but did not stop until we got into town.

The first officer of whom Gertrude asked directions turned out to be Tarn McGrew, an old friend whom we used to meet at the Jacots. He said to Gertrude, I will have two of my men watch over your car and you will come and talk to a group of soldiers who have already arrived and who must be informed of what they should know about the French. That evening they all wanted to know how far they were from the front, expecting to hear cannons and see dead Germans.

One of the soldiers said to Gertrude, There are very nice young ladies in this town, one of them has been spending the afternoon with me. And Gertrude said, They are not ladies if she spent an afternoon with you.

The next morning we were off for Paris where we received our new assignment, which was Nîmes. The committee gave us a letter of introduction to the head of the military hospital there, and we drove south again. When we arrived at Nîmes and presented our credentials, the wife of the chief surgeon of the hospital asked if we could come to her home the following afternoon to meet some of the doctors stationed in town. We went to Madame Fabre's home, where the doctors and some of their wives were sitting around a large tea table. Madame Fabre asked me if in San Francisco there were many French inhabitants and I said, Twenty-five percent of the population are of French descent. Do they remain good French people? she asked. And I said, To the extent that there are some who send their daughters back to the Sacred Heart in Paris for their schooling. Madame Fabre turned her back upon me. It was then I realized that she was of a Protestant family. Later, however, we became good friends.

At the station in Nîmes there had been arranged a reception area for wounded soldiers. Two nuns were preparing to receive them and serve them hot drinks, and Gertrude came to help. The nuns had put on the stove a huge cauldron of chocolate with the typical army tin cups to serve it in, and I had brought supplies and cigarettes. By this time there was little tobacco either for army or civilian use, so these cigarettes were precious. In the hospitals the soldiers smoked what they pulled out of their mattresses.

We went regularly to the station to get the supplies that arrived. One day we were notified that a load of supplies was going to waste at the station and we should come at once. We went and I saw the stationmaster, telling him that the supplies were Red Cross supplies and not intended for us, how could I accept them? Ah, he said, it is the carelessness of the American Red Cross that permits this waste.

We had become acquainted with and devoted to Madame Thibon, the wife of the Préfet of the Gard. She was thoroughly discouraged with the American Red Cross and said, You should do something about it. But we said it was not our responsibility.

Madame Thibon had a handsome son whom I supposed was escaping military service. Madame Thibon later informed me he was too young to serve, but that he had gotten his parents' permission to go to the war as soon as he turned eighteen. I had done Jacques a great injustice.

One day we went to Marseilles where Gertrude got oil and tires for her automobile from the military park. There at a little restaurant, where the food was extraordinarily good, the waiter asked me if there was anything I wanted and I replied, Yes, cigarettes. Before we departed he brought me a mysterious parcel wrapped with newspaper and said, Here they are. When I paid the modest bill for the lunch I asked him how much I owed for the cigarettes. He said, They were included, madame, in the bill.

At Christmas we went from Nîmes to Aix-en-Provence to visit the hospitals and to give a party for the stray English soldiers stationed there. Several English governesses from Perpignan had driven over with provisions for a dinner. As it was very cold we proposed staying overnight at the hotel and driving back to Nîmes the following morning. Miss Larkins, the prettiest of the English girls, said to me when the party was over, The officer in the bedroom next to the one I am occupy-

ing, when I went into mine he knocked at the wall and said,
'Shall I light my fire?' To which I said, I hope you did not answer. Oh no, she said, of course I did not.

At the station we met one day Sir Hugh Munro with his two
daughters, who were directing a distribution of English supplies at Tarascon. Carmen, the younger daughter, was small
and lively. Her sister was tall with immense dignity and wore
very large diamond earrings that contrasted curiously with her
blue cotton Red Cross uniform.

At the same time that we met the Munros we met an English
Quaker, Coventry, who immediately became infatuated with
both the Misses Munro. He had served with the Serbian army
and had as a friend in Nîmes Matitch, a Serbian officer who had
been a law student in Aix-en-Provence. We took them to the
hospitals we visited, having them sit on the step of the car.
When we got onto a road that needed repair, Matitch would
jump off like a bird to balance the car.

Gertrude and I asked them if they would like to go on a
picnic lunch which I would provide. Matitch said, Oh thank
you, but no. The Americans love eating out-of-doors, but all
I ask is to have a roof over my head.

Sir Hugh Munro asked Gertrude if she were interested in
pictures and she laughed and said, I have a large collection of
modern pictures. Sir Hugh said, Mine are not modern but I
have a large collection. What painters have you? She told him
and he said, Mine are Titians, Rubens', Rembrandts. Carmen
while her father was speaking said to me, Nobody knows about
them in England because the family has never paid taxes on
them.

It was announced that American soldiers were to be stationed near Nîmes. The land for their camp had been selected.

They were Southern soldiers and already there were Negro soldiers arriving. Gertrude said to Dr. Fabre, There will be trouble between the Southerners and the Negroes. What do you mean? asked Dr. Fabre. They do not love each other, said Gertrude. That, said Dr. Fabre, I find very little civilized.

Each day the war news was more encouraging. The Allies were advancing toward Strasbourg. To our surprise one morning, the armistice was announced. I was shocked. Were the Germans beaten? I was dropping tears of relief. Compose yourself, said Gertrude. You have no right to show a tearful countenance to the French whose sons will no longer be killed.

A wire from Mrs. Lathrop asked if we spoke German. If we did, we should close up the depot at once and return to Paris to prepare to open a depot for civilian relief in Alsace. There was no hesitation in my reply. We both spoke German and would be in Paris as quickly as possible.

I gave the remaining bandages and supplies to a nun who was returning to Jerusalem. The nuns had been asked to work in the French hospitals during the war, but after the war these nuns did not have enough money to pay for the privilege of wearing their habits as the French government required. The nun took the provisions I gave her and gave me some little medals in return, which I kept until the Germans took them during the Second War.

In Paris, where we stayed briefly, Gertrude and I each bought a fur-lined aviator's jacket and a knitted sweater. Then we packed the car and went off one icy morning for Alsace. We spent the first night at a small hotel where we were given the room that Miss Margaret Wilson, our President's daughter, was to occupy the next night. I was warned that I was not to drop anything on the floor, neither perfume nor talcum powder nor face powder, for they would not have time to sweep before her arrival in the morning.

That afternoon we got into a mix-up on the road with the French army, which was, like us, on the way to Alsace. The horses of the kitchen wagon had become unruly and collided with the car, bending the steering gear under the car and breaking the tool chest which was outside on the step. I got out and gathered together the tools. The horses had also broken a window of the car so by the time we got to Nancy, the car weaving and wandering all over the road, I was disgracefully covered with mud.

At Nancy we went to the headquarters of our society, where they welcomed us very kindly but were aghast at the condition we were in. We had a light supper, went to bed, slept, and got up early and toured the battlefield. We lunched at a famous deluxe restaurant, Weber, and in the afternoon went on our way to Mulhouse, which was to be our future headquarters.

We were at once in no man's land. The road was desolate and bare, and the fan belt on the truck was broken. Gertrude thought that she would mend it with a hairpin, but that was not successful. At that moment, on the road facing us was a French military car. Gertrude hailed it. I saw at once that a soldier was driving the car but that on the seat back of him were two generals. I said to Gertrude, Carefully my dear, he is a general. I do not care, said Gertrude.

The soldier asked permission from his officers to put the car in order, and they nodded their consent. The driver came up and looked at the car and said, Oh I have something that will hold that better than a hairpin. In no time he had tightened the fan belt and put it back in place. I had a supply of cigarettes from the British Red Cross from which I drew a sufficient quantity to express my thanks.

At Mulhouse we had several letters of introduction, one to the French director in charge of hospitals who thought we should put ourselves in the hands of the chief surgeon there who could help us to find a suitable hotel. The hotel we had chosen was excellent but was being requisitioned for French officers and we could not go there any more. A little Alsatian hotel was recommended, where we settled and stayed that winter.

We began our distribution of clothing to the Alsatians who were returning to their homes from Germany, to which they had been evacuated by the Germans during the war. We were given a large gymnasium for our use where we unpacked and from which we were to distribute. Gertrude spoke a fluent incorrect German which the Alsatians understood. I tried to remember the correct German I had been taught. I heard an Alsatian woman who was waiting to give me her list say to her neighbor, She is a Prussian. Gertrude was delighted.

Amongst the people who came to see us was a Miss Schimmel. She was a very old-fashioned young Alsatian and Gertrude made a rhyme, Himmel Himmel here comes Schimmel. She was always interrupting us but she was very kind and very helpful. Her brother had escaped from Alsace and had joined and fought in the French army.

One day on the road something was making a noise in the engine of the car. Gertrude got out to see what it was. At that moment two American soldiers passed by and asked if they could help. Gertrude said, Yes, I do not think it is serious but there is a little noise. Whereupon they got down on their knees and before you knew it they had taken the engine down, looked it over, brushed all the parts and put them back again. This did not take them any time at all. Gertrude and I were astonished.

In the late spring, going back to Paris from Mulhouse, we stopped over to see Mildred Aldrich. Mildred was surprised and pleased to see us, and we exchanged all our experiences of the war. Mildred's servant confided to us that during the war Miss Aldrich had given away all the money she had earned from her best-selling book, *A Hilltop on the Marne*. She had given it to the hilltop from which she said she had earned it, to the wounded in the little hospital, to the families of the men that had been wounded or killed.

The following day, after lunch, we returned to Paris. The city, like us, was sadder than when we left it.

7

GERTRUDE's Ford had been transformed into something that Frank Jacot said resembled a second-class hearse, and he now advised Gertrude to get a new two-seated Ford at once. We went out to the Ford factory and ordered one. In a very short while we were notified that it had arrived. Gertrude very proudly drove it. We sat very high. As before the war, nothing but private cars were being allowed in the Bois.

One day, about this time, we got into a traffic jam on the boulevard Saint Germain near the church of St. Germain-des-

Prés. I saw Gertrude bowing very politely to a man who had
taken off his hat and had bowed to her. I had not had time to
see his face. I said to her, Who was that? and Gertrude answered, Leo. She had not heard from him or of him during the
war years. I said, Not possibly. And she said, Yes, it was Leo.
Gertrude when we got home wrote her story, "How She Bowed
to Her Brother." Leo still had his beautiful walk, which was
not historical but mythological.

I had no servant but a *femme de ménage* who was strange,
not very cheerful, a good worker though slightly deformed in
body. She asked, to my surprise, if she might make *visitan-
dines,* and I naturally gave my consent. I was more curious
than hopeful. She proceeded to mix the dough. I did not interrupt her, but it seemed to me that she was not going about it
quite right. Then she said, When anything goes wrong in my
cooking I pray, I ask the Virgin to help me, and I have known
a curdled mayonnaise to come out all right. I thought that
while she retired to pray she neglected her cooking, so that
prayer was necessary.

Our home was filled with friends. Amongst the painters was
Marcoussis, who returning from the front had bought himself
a small car. In a jam at the Place de l'Opéra he stood up in it
and began directing the traffic, the policeman had either not
yet returned from the war or had been killed at the front. He
was succeeding fairly well when a man called out, Who are
you that you should order us about? Who am I? said Marcoussis. It was I who gave you back Alsace and Lorraine.

Just how we had come to meet Elmer Harden I do not know,
but he now was a frequent visitor. He was a great reader, he
could learn anything by heart, he knew all of *Paradise Lost.*

Harden had returned from the war and was studying music.

He told us that when he got to the front there were already some Americans killed and wounded on the field and he heard a French officer cry out, Lead them around the other way so they will not walk on their own dead and wounded.

Harden later fell seriously in love with La Argentina. He never spoke to her though he saw her every day. When she died, he went every morning to the cemetery to put flowers on her grave.

Harden went everywhere together with his great friend Pierre. Years later they came down and looked at the flat in the rue Christine before we moved there. The carpets had been cut but not laid yet, and Elmer and Pierre saw them with the tools of the working men on the floor. Harden said, What is this? You are not laying carpets on this wonderful floor? It was what they call parquet de Versailles. I said, Oh yes I am, I am not going to repair spots on the waxed floors any more, and besides the carpet will be warmer. Harden said, It is criminal, I forbid you to do it Alice, it is criminal. And Pierre said, being more polite, Oh please do not. I said, I cannot have a man in every day to wax the floors. Harden said, Oh I will pay him, do not think of that.

Kate Buss came from the same town as Elmer – Medford, Massachusetts. She was very pretty, not young, very gay. She had a long flirtation with Ezra Pound which Gertrude tried to discourage.

As I remember, she spent a year in Paris at that time and was more or less fiancée to either an Egyptian or a Turk. She had the lovely name of Kate Meldram Buss but Kate Buss was Shakespearian enough.

Kate Buss brought Alfred Kreymborg to see Gertrude Stein. Kreymborg and Harold Loeb had come over from New York to publish some numbers of *Broom* in Paris. Harold Loeb was the son of very rich people and had enough money to do this. Kreymborg was a gentle poetic soul.

After a few numbers, they moved to Rome. Somebody said at the time, The little magazines were born to make verse free.

Jacques Lipchitz was successively a Russian and a Pole, according to wars that he went through. He came to France, settled there and took out French nationality.

Lipchitz had made a portrait of Jean Cocteau, and now he made one of Gertrude Stein. During a hot summer, she went every day and posed for him in his studio where the sun poured down.

His wife, Berthe, was a very good cook and asked us several times to dine with them in the studio. One day I went to call for Gertrude. I walked up the steep stairs and, turning, I saw Berthe coming down the stairs and got out of her way to give her room because it was a narrow stairway. I said how do you do to her. But she paid no attention to me, it was exactly as though she had not seen or heard me and did not know I was there. Sometimes I used to think that it was a witchery that came over her from the African ivory and wood jewelry which Lipchitz found for her.

One year Lipchitz had from a friend an invitation to go down to Palma de Mallorca, and as he was leaving Paris he noticed two early Gothic heads at the antiquity shop on the ground floor of the studio building where he lived. As he had not a sou he could not buy them, so he carefully hid them behind two old armchairs so that no one would find them until his return. When, having been paid for an elegant piece of sculpture of a toreador, he returned to Paris with the money he had earned, he went directly to the antiquity shop, uncovered the two pieces of sculpture and bought them.

Sherwood Anderson came from Chicago to Paris with his second wife, Tennessee, and Paul Rosenfeld. Sylvia Beach brought the three of them to see Gertrude at Sherwood's request. I can remember Tennessee sitting on the big table in the studio, listening to what the others were saying without taking part in the conversation herself.

That was the first time Sherwood came to Paris. After they were back in Chicago, he and Tennessee were divorced.

The next time Sherwood came to Paris he was with his third wife, Elizabeth Prall. They had brought with them two of Sherwood's children by his first wife. When someone on the boat asked Mimi, who was beautiful and looked like her father, how her mother took her tea, she said, I am sure I do not know. They had not met before going on the boat.

John, the young son of Sherwood Anderson, was about to become a painter. When after a short while his father, stepmother, and Mimi returned to America, he suddenly became independent and a painter. On the day of their departure he woke up to the fact. He came to see Gertrude frequently and she became attached to him.

Ralph Church came to us through Sherwood Anderson. Mrs. Church, his mother, was very beautiful but Sherwood said, She makes me nervous. She used to send Gertrude the most beautiful yellow roses. At the time of Gertrude's death an horticulturist in New Jersey was creating a yellow rose for her. They never were yellow enough. They should be yellow, large, and fragrant, she said.

Ralph Church was a philosopher who had undertaken to secure a doctorate of philosophy at Oxford. When Hemingway

came to Paris, Sherwood Anderson gave him letters of introduction to Church and to Gertrude. Church made no effort to
see Hemingway and did not ask Gertrude anything about him.
Later Gertrude said to Church, Church let me see your hand.
And then she said surprised, But you have enormous curiosity,
how is it you have made no effort to hear about Hemingway?
Well, said Church, I am waiting to make up my mind myself
concerning him. They never became friends, Church and Hemingway.

Shortly after the war the Willie Dunbar Jewetts came back
to Paris on a visit and we went over to their hotel to see them.
There, on different occasions, we met a very redheaded young
man and a very black-haired young man, Robert Coates and
Man Ray.

Man Ray looked like an Indian potentate in miniature, very
pretentious. Which he was not at all, he was simple. He was
making his way and said to Gertrude, Will you pose for me? I
would like to take a photograph of you. As usual she said, Certainly. She always said she would try anything once.

Man Ray gave her the address of his hotel in the rue De-
lambre. The room where he proposed to take the photograph
was a little cubicle, a hall bedroom in a small hotel, but there
he had all his cameras and wires and lights of all degrees. He
took there the first of many photographs of Gertrude, a very
nice one.

From that day on Man Ray took so many photographs of
Gertrude that one day laughingly he said, I am your official
photographer. And when he saw a snapshot I had taken of her
in a field he was angry and said he thought he was her official
photographer, what was I doing in this affair?

Eventually Man Ray went back to America and only came on visits to Paris.

Gertrude became quite attached to Robert Coates. He had a pretty, velvety voice and gentle ways. One day he brought Gertrude his first book, *The Eater of Darkness*. That was a tragedy because Virgil Thomson borrowed it, the only copy naturally that Gertrude had which was inscribed, and promptly lost it. I saw Virgil's advertisement for it in the New York *Herald* and said to Gertrude, But he must find it. However, he did not.

It is only within the last few years that Coates sent me a reprint of the book from America. It is quite as good as I remembered, indeed better – thrilling, intense and dramatic. In the years between, of course, he has written many excellent novels, and his art news and short stories have appeared in *The New Yorker*. They all are distinguished.

Later he came over to Rome where I was and I met him again. His wife danced marvelously with our host.

Gertrude and I were frequently visited by our good friend Mildred Aldrich, and now we learned that a small annuity she had had suddenly ceased. We found that it was not a gift of the person we had thought. An old beau and his rich wife had been giving it. We got a man who was a good friend of these people to ask why it had ceased. The answer was, My wife in her old age has had an attack of parsimony and I myself am on her reduced list and cannot even use the cars in the garage. I have to walk to the station if I want to go into New York.

We made a systematic combing of everyone we knew to try to find somebody who could supply the money needed for Mildred. All during that hot summer we struggled to find the

necessary funds. Finally it was decided that Gertrude should
appeal to the editor of the *Atlantic Monthly*. Unfortunately,
he had the bad taste of putting a paragraph in the magazine.
But he got subscriptions, and one young woman subscribed
five hundred dollars and came to see us in Paris saying, If that
is not enough I can always give more.

Mildred was of course outraged at becoming a public bene-
ficiary. She told Gertrude that when she first knew the annuity
had ceased she had written to the librarian of the American
Library in Paris, saying that he should come at once to take her
books because she did not know if she was going to be able to
stay on at the Hilltop. Gertrude now went to speak to the
librarian about this and he said, If she will give us her books
at her death we will take care of them until then. Which Mildred accepted.

There was, at least until lately, a Mildred Aldrich room at
the library where her books were gathered together. She had a
great many, some of them were of considerable value because
they were first editions or were out-of-print. Her letters that
she had kept – she had torn up many – she told Gertrude were to
go to her.

William Cook used to go out in his little car to Mildred's and
bring her in to spend the holidays – Christmas, New Year's,
Thanksgiving and the Fourth of July. He said Mildred was an
interesting old lady but a difficult guest.

One day Amelie, Mildred's servant, telephoned that Miss
Aldrich had had a heart attack. She always spent the night
alone in the house, Amelie came in the morning. When Amelie
got there she had found Mildred on the floor. Amelie had sent
for the local doctor.

Gertrude telephoned to Cook and the three of us went out

there. Cook thought that the best care would be given Mildred at the American Hospital at Neuilly. Mildred was tenderly cared for there but died shortly afterward. Cook and Gertrude arranged for the funeral.

Mildred had had the habit of wearing on her nightdress her Légion d'honneur. She was very proud of having received it. At the funeral an officer in uniform wearing a great many medals represented the Légion d'honneur.

There were a great many flowers, which Mildred would have enjoyed. She was buried at the little cemetery at Huiry.

Ford Madox Ford came over to Paris to establish *The Trans-atlantic Review.* Thereafter, he came to see Gertrude frequently. I had a weakness for him. Hemingway called him the golden walrus.

One afternoon we went to see him and, like a good Frenchman, he had a gathering of young poets. He said to Gertrude, How many of these do you know? Pointing her stick to Harold Loeb she said, Up to there. Get up, said Ford, and bow to Miss Gertrude Stein.

When he was looking for a little house in the country I suggested Guermantes, where he did find a wee house with a wee garden where he planted a good many flowers. He said to me, When you ask a French person what that flower is, they usually answer mignonette. The great château of Guermantes, the château of Proust's hero, was within easy walking distance of the little house.

The whole story of Ford Madox Ford and Violet Hunt would have been comic if it had not been tragic. We met them at Alice Ullman's before the First World War when they were returning from Germany, where Violet Hunt believed herself to have been married to Ford. He was, however, married to a wife in northern England. When Violet Hunt discovered what he had done, she wrote her book and at a party at Harry Phelan Gibb's she took me aside and said, Do you know what a dreadful thing Ford Madox Ford did to me? And I had to acknowledge that I did, I had read her book with the most intense excitement. Undoubtedly Ford was amusing but he made trouble for Violet Hunt.

One day there was a party where we met for the first time Mary and Louis Bromfield. Hemingway was amongst the young men present. Ford was talking to Gertrude when Hemingway came up to speak to her. Ford wafted him away saying, Go away young man, it is I who am speaking to Miss Stein, do not interrupt me. And he then asked Gertrude if he might dedicate his new book to her. Gertrude was very touched and I was delighted.

The next to the last time I saw Ford was one evening when he came to the rue de Fleurus with a very pretty redheaded girl and said to me, Alice tell her she should marry me. I, knowing the circumstances of his real marriage, said, Oh Ford I cannot. He said, Oh yes you can, tell her now. As she came from Baltimore, it was complicating things for Gertrude. I said nothing more to the girl and Ford let the subject drop for a moment. Then he came to me and said, I shall go over to Baltimore to explain to her parents what I want and they will allow me to marry their daughter. Which of course they could not do.

At about this time Lady Rothermere invited Gertrude and me to a reception she was giving in Paris for T.S. Eliot. Gertrude was not eager to go but I had told Lady Rothermere that we would. So I started to make an evening dress, as all my prewar clothes had worn out. I was finishing the dress the afternoon of November fifteenth when Lady Rothermere and Eliot came to the rue de Fleurus. I hastily gathered my dress together and rolled it up.

T.S. Eliot wanted to ask Gertrude some questions about her writing and she said, Yes, go ahead. He said, Can you tell me, Miss Stein, what authority you have for so frequently using the split infinitive? Henry James, said Gertrude.

Eliot at that time was the editor of *The Criterion,* which was supported by Lady Rothermere. He said to Gertrude, We would very much like to have an article of yours. Yes? said Gertrude. But, said Eliot, it must be your very latest thing. Yes, said Gertrude. And they left.

That evening Gertrude wrote a portrait of T.S. Eliot which she called "The Fifteenth of November," so that there could be no doubt but that it was her very latest thing. It did not appear in the next number of *The Criterion* nor the one after nor the one after that, so that Gertrude commenced telling everybody, He is afraid to publish it. Whether this ever got to his ears or not we did not know, but she did not hesitate to say that he was quick to ask for an article but not so quick to publish it.

We had first met Lady Rothermere at a party she had given for Muriel Draper, to which we had gone because we were fond of Muriel. There, we were introduced to Miss Natalie Barney and Miss Romaine Brooks. It was probably at the Russian ballet that we met these ladies again and Miss Barney asked us to come to one of her Friday afternoon teas, which was the beginning of a long and warm friendship.

Romaine Brooks was a portrait painter who had painted several portraits of D'Annunzio, one of which had been bought by the French government and was in the Luxembourg Gallery. She had at that time a flat in Paris on the Quai de Conti. It was furnished in the style of that period – a great deal of black, a black floor, black furniture covers. It was somber but with a great deal of taste.

At Natalie Barney's there were many comfortable chairs and a very large round table where tea was served. The room gave on a shady garden with many trees but no flowers. On the other side of the pavillon was a small passageway to a temple of friendship.

At her teas there was always a large and mixed gathering of academicians, writers and a few painters. Marie Laurencin was frequently there. Natalie Barney's sister, whom we had met at Nîmes during the war, spoke very prettily at an afternoon *Hommage à Gertrude* that Miss Barney had arranged.

When we moved to the rue Christine Miss Barney used to sign herself, Your friend and nearest neighbor, for the rue Jacob is not more than four blocks away from the rue Christine.

It was Natalie Barney who introduced us to the Duchess de Clermont-Tonnerre. Gertrude and the Duchess became good friends. It was a friendship that lasted until Gertrude's death.

Scott Fitzgerald was brought to us in Paris by Hemingway one evening in 1925, just after *The Great Gatsby* was published. Hemingway brought both Fitzgerald and Zelda. Fitzgerald brought a copy of his book.

Scott, who was not averse to giving Hem a little dig, once came up to me and said, Miss Toklas I am sure you want to hear how Hem achieves his great moments. And Hem said rather bashfully, What are you up to Scotty? He said, You tell her. And Hem said, Well, you see, it is this way, When I have an idea I turn down the flame, as if it were a little alcohol stove, as low as it will go. Then it explodes and that is my idea. Fitzgerald turned his back on this and I said, The retreat from Caporetto is well done. I did not say anything about the rest of the book and Hem was satisfied.

Fitzgerald continued to see Gertrude. There used to be a good deal of talk about his drinking, but he was always sober when he came to the house. One afternoon he said, You know I am thirty years old today and it is tragic. What is to become of me, what am I to do? And Gertrude told him that he should not worry, that he had been writing like a man of thirty for many years. She told him that he would go home and write a greater novel than he ever had. She had thought very well of *This Side of Paradise* and *The Great Gatsby*. When *Tender Is the Night* was published he sent a copy to Gertrude with the inscription, Is this the book you asked for?

Amongst the visitors at rue de Fleurus were the Paul Robesons, who came over to Paris with a letter from Carl Van Vechten. They were on their way to Villefranche. Gertrude said to me, We have to give them a party. So she commenced asking people, having asked the Robesons to come earlier than five o'clock.

When they came, Gertrude took them into the dining room to take off their coats and hats. Mrs. Robeson had in her hand a very heavy leather bag. She said, At the last moment there were things I had to buy and I slipped them all into this bag. Razors, you know.

The party went off very nicely and Robeson asked Gertrude if the guests would like him to sing. She said, Oh of course they would. So he sang several spirituals.

One day when a little American woman was at the house, Robeson was there. It was something of a contretemps as she was so very Southern. She asked Robeson, You are from the

South, are you not? Oh no, said Robeson, I was born and raised in New Jersey. What a pity, said she. Not for me, said Robeson.

Edith Sitwell came to see Gertrude through the editor of the London *Vogue*, whom we had met in Paris and who had told Gertrude that Edith Sitwell wanted to meet her. Earlier, Miss Sitwell had written an article on Gertrude's work for a London magazine, not too enthusiastic. The following year she wrote one for *Vogue*, she was enthusiastic, she had changed her mind.

She was brought to the house by Elmer Harden. Miss Sitwell was a great surprise to us for she looked like nobody under the sun, very tall, rather the height of a grenadier, with marked features and the most beautiful nose any woman had. She was a gendarme, she wore double-breasted coats with large buttons. It was the beginning of a long friendship.

Miss Sitwell said that Gertrude should come to England to lecture at Cambridge. Then came an invitation from Oxford. Gertrude wrote her lecture on the seat of her Ford car while it was being mended in the garage. When she came home she said, Well, I have done it. I have written my lecture. And she told me how and where and when.

She was somewhat disturbed about reading her lectures and asked various people what she should do. One day at Natalie Barney's Gertrude asked the advice of a very charming professor. He said, Read as quickly as you can, never look up, use a low voice. Another acquaintance, Prichard, said, Speak as slowly as you can, as loudly as you can, and never look down.

In the spring we went over to England. In London the Sitwells were giving a reading of the poetry of Edith, Osbert and Sacheverell, and Gertrude had been asked by them to sit on the platform. So that I was left alone for a moment when Dolly

Wilde came up and said to me, Alice, where is darling Gertrude? I said, Darling Dolly, she is on the platform.

At Cambridge Gertrude had a quiet and intense audience. She had no difficulty in keeping their attention. After the lecture the men in the audience asked a great many questions. The women, however, said nothing.

At Oxford we lunched with Harold Acton and then were led by the Sitwells to the room where Gertrude was to lecture. There was a large, attentive, quiet audience that became lively and amused after the lecture when they commenced to ask questions. The Sitwells were astonished at Gertrude's quick answers and wit. They wanted us to extend our English stay, but we went by railroad that evening to London and were home the following day.

8

IN the summer of 1922 we had gone down to Saint-Rémy, situated in the valley of the Rhône, and we had spent the summer, fall and winter there. When winter came the mistral blew, the hotel was cold. One day we went out to a little village on the hills and sat down there, hoping to be protected against the wind. We were on a plowed field hard with the cold air, and I could not walk on it. Suddenly I found myself crying. Gertrude said, What is the matter? The weather, I said, can we go back to Paris? She said, Tomorrow.

But Gertrude had written so well there, and so happily and so much, that I made up my mind I would behave and not complain.

A few years later we were intending to visit Picasso at Antibes when we stopped to spend a night or two at Pernollet's hotel at Belley. Madame Pernollet brought up to our rooms some garden flowers – they looked like flowers out of a garden, they did not look like a florist's flowers. We said, Oh how perfectly charming, have you a garden here? She said, No, what you see out of the back window is a vegetable garden, there are practically no flowers there. But there are plenty of gardens around here, and we get our flowers from them. You must walk up and look at the flowers in Monsieur Genevrey's garden. Monsieur Genevrey is an horticulturist.

So we went there that afternoon and got some more flowers and had a conversation with Monsieur Fred Genevrey. He was the oldest in the family but would have been the head in any case from his manner. He took charge of us and we looked at his place and saw the view of the valley below. Occasionally Mont Blanc was visible.

We had supposed when we arrived in Belley that we would only be there for a night or two, but the country was fascinating. As we drove around the countryside we became more and more enthusiastic and made no attempts to join Picasso on the Riviera but wired him, Are staying on here at least for the present. Later Gertrude wrote to him that we would be staying in Belley for the summer.

One day Monsieur Genevrey, when we went to get some flowers, told us that the Baroness Pierlot had asked to meet us. If we would drive over to Béon, across the valley, he would bicycle to her château and meet us there. Which we and he did. The Baroness became a good friend.

In 1870 Madame Pierlot had been brought by her father from Lyon, their city home, to Béon to escape the horrors of the war. Her third son had been killed as a young man in the First World War. Now her first and second husbands were both dead. The first was an army man who had been a military attaché in Switzerland and in Rome, the second a Napoleonic baron who had inherited a considerable fortune and was director of the museum at Creil. She remembered everything. Gertrude used to say she had a memory that rivaled mine. But she had things to remember.

Near the château at Béon was a small seventeenth-century house called the Cellier – cellar – where the wine was made. Madame Pierlot proposed that Gertrude should install herself there in the afternoons, or even all day, to work quietly where there should be no disturbance.

After several summers at Belley we saw a house at Bilignin where we wanted to spend our summers. We had not found anything until one day from the valley below we saw the house at Bilignin and Gertrude said, I will drive you up there and you can go and tell them that we will take their house. I said, But it may not be for rent. She said, The curtains are floating out the windows. Well, I said, I think that proves someone is living there.

But I arranged to have a conversation with the agent of the owner of the house. He told me that the present occupant was an officer in the army but that it might soon be necessary for the officer's regiment to move. If that event occurred, it would be possible for us to sublet the house and finally have a lease directly from the owner.

Finally the regiment left. We signed a paper giving us the house, without seeing it nearer than from the road. We and our white poodle, Basket, moved in and settled down.

For years after reading *The Princess Casamassima* I had wanted a white poodle. One day at the dog show in Paris Gertrude saw a pair of white poodles with a puppy and the puppy jumped into her arms. We spoke to the woman who owned them and she said, The puppy is for sale, the mother has had a bad pregnancy and I have spent a great deal of money at the vet's. Gertrude said we would take him, but would the woman keep him until he was housebroken? So she took him back and said we could call for him in two weeks.

We went out to get him a few days before we were leaving for Belley. That night Georges Hugnet came to see us and said, What dog is it that is crying? We said, The pup we have bought. He said, Oh bring him down, do not let him cry. Georges was enchanted with Basket.

We named him Basket because I had said he should carry a basket of flowers in his mouth. Which he never did.

Earlier than that I had wanted a Bedlington and we had all but bought one in London when we went to see John Lane, but as war was declared at that time we could not take a dog into France. When we finally took to spending our summers at Belley I said, Basket a Bedlington at Belley would be the proper name. But it was not a Bedlington it was a poodle.

Basket was the beginning of a succession of dogs, which included Byron, Pépé and Basket II. Byron was a Chihuahua, a gift from Picabia whose Chihuahua we had admired.

The night Byron arrived, Gertrude and I alternately kept him in our laps and when it was time to go to bed Basket could not be found. He had gone out to the gate to try to escape the jealousy that was gnawing at him. When we discovered this, Gertrude and I both ran out and brought him back, trying not to let him be jealous any more.

One day at Bilignin Picasso and his wife, with Elf their Airedale dog, came up in their big car – they had a big limousine with a chauffeur. They had come to spend the day with us. They got out of the car and we thought they were a circus. They were wearing the winter sports clothes of southern France, which had not gotten to America yet and were a novelty to us – bare legs, bare arms, bright clothes. Pablo said, explaining himself, That is all right, it is done down on the Mediterranean.

Elf ran over the box hedges of the terrace flower beds. Basket looked at the dog with the same scandal with which we had looked at her masters. Basket was outraged, he had never been allowed to do that.

We received numerous visitors in the country, amongst them Carl Van Vechten and Henry McBride. Carl, of course, we had known since before the war. We had first seen him at the second performance of "Le Sacre du Printemps." He sat in the same box we were in and I said to Gertrude, Be careful not to speak English, he certainly understands English. Later I said, I think he is our guest of tomorrow evening. He was.

Carl had been on the staff in Paris of the New York *Times* until he gave it up one day and went back to New York to write. He wrote about music mostly at that time, Mary Garden was a great enthusiasm of his. He had a good deal the position as an authority that Virgil Thomson had a generation later. Then one day he began writing novels. His *Nigger Heaven* had an enormous success and influence. It with "Melanctha" were the two great stories about Negroes.

Carl was a reformed character after the death of Avery Hopwood. It had been a terrible shock to him. Avery Hopwood and Carl Van Vechten together had created modern New York. They changed everything to their way of seeing and doing. It became as gay, irresponsible and brilliant as they were.

Carl had sent Avery to us when he was in Paris and we adored him. Gertrude said that he had the air of a sheep with the possibility of being a wolf. His blond head fell to one side heavily. He loved Gertrude. It was he who brought Gertrude Atherton to the house, he said he wanted his two Gertrudes to meet.

One night Avery invited us to dinner and Beverley Nichols was the other guest. He contradicted Avery on some point of no particular importance and Avery said, Hush young man, you and your opinions mean nothing in my young life. Of a sudden Avery took out from his pocket a small paper and emptied a white powder into the palm of his hand and swallowed it. Gertrude knew more about this than I did and said, Oh Avery, you must not. But it was too late.

When the maitre d'hôtel brought the bill Avery wafted him away. Gertrude said, Is that effective, Avery? And he said, Well not always, but I always do it.

One night he took us to Florence's cabaret. She said to Gertrude, He does not like paying his bill, he comes before he leaves Paris to ask me how much he owes me and he writes me a check. That is one way of avoiding knowing how much anything costs.

The last time we saw Avery, some years later, he called for us and gathered in cars and taxis a large number of companions. We had dinner in Montmartre and visited various places. Avery and Gertrude and I were in one taxi and Avery said, in

"It begins like this: 'gertrude says four hats is a hat is a hat.' What the hell can you make out of a declaration like that, chief?"

"In the autumn of 1934 we went from New York to Chicago, to settle a misunderstanding as to what and where Gertrude Stein was to lecture." *—Photographed by Carl Van Vechten*

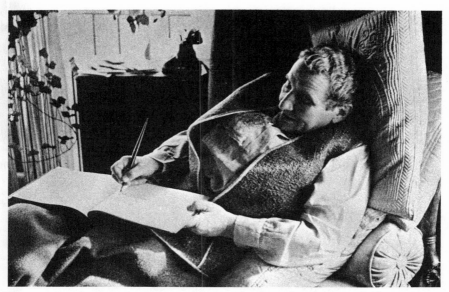

Gertrude Stein in Chicago. "Bobsy Goodspeed, whom we had seen
in France, received us in her home . . ."

". . . Mrs. Goodspeed gave a tea party for Gertrude Stein to meet a great
number of her friends." (*Below*) Miss Toklas, Bobsy Goodspeed and
Fanny Butcher (*standing*), Claire Dux Swift (*seated*) and Gertrude Stein.

(*Left to right*) Robert Hutchins, Claire Dux Swift, Thornton Wilder and Mrs. Maude Phelps Hutchins in April, 1935.

W. G. Rogers' picture of Gertrude Stein, with horse and buggy, at Springfield, Massachusetts, early in 1935.

—*Photographed by Carl Van Vechten*

"With Carl Van Vechten we went to Richmond," where Gertrude Stein was photographed viewing a seventeenth-century house.

—*Photographed by Carl Van Vechten*

Students surrounded Gertrude Stein after her lecture at Williamsburg, Virginia, early in 1935.

The frozen fountain in the garden of the Poe Foundation of Richmond, Virginia, early 1935.

Fania Marinoff Van Vechten, Gertrude Stein and Alice Toklas. "Carl took some perfect photographs of Gertrude with her many waistcoats as a background."

Carl Van Vechten and
Gertrude Stein aboard the
S.S. *Champlain* in May, 1935.

—Wide World Photos

At Faringdon House in England in 1936. The group includes (*left to right, back row*) Lord Berners, Lady Rosebery, Lady Bridget Parsons, Sir Robert Abdy; (*front row*) Lady Diana Abdy, Mr. Robert Heber-Percy, Alice Toklas and Gertrude Stein.

—Photographed by Bobsy Goodspeed Chapman

Thornton Wilder and Gertrude Stein at Bilignin, the summer of 1935.

Basket II with
Gertrude Stein at Bilignin,
the winter of 1939-1940.

In the 1940's, riding in the Bois de Boulogne.

Portrait of Gertrude Stein by Cecil Beaton. ▶

—Photographed by E. Sottsass

Alice B. Toklas at the rue Christine in 1951.

speaking of a friend of his, He will get the best of me yet. He will kill me. Gertrude said, Do not talk like that, Avery, you do not have to be killed. And Avery said, He is pursuing me and he will kill me.

Gertrude and I drove down to Belley the next day and after a little while there was a postal card from Avery thanking us for coming to his party. But there was no stamp on the card, it was Avery's little way of getting things done for him without any bother. That very day we had news that Avery had been drowned in the Mediterranean.

Henry McBride fortunately had come to stay for a few days and that distracted Gertrude from the shock and sadness of Avery's death.

Jane Heap and Margaret Anderson had come to Paris in the early twenties to publish *The Little Review,* which they had begun in Chicago, and it was Jane Heap who now introduced to us a young Russian painter, Pavlik Tchelitchev. His painting interested Gertrude for a little while. Until it went bad, as she said. Then his paintings were moved into the *salon des refusés.*

It was through Tchelitchev that we met René Crevel. René Crevel of all the young men was the only one I really loved. I adored him. He was blue-eyed and demi-blond, with irregular features that made him look like a sailor. He spoke very quickly and brilliantly and made sharp gestures. He was, alas, tubercular. His mother, the unhappy widow of a well-known editor of music who had made his fortune publishing the Boulanger march, would not recognize that René required special care for his health until it got so bad that an operation was necessary.

René and Tchelitchev's sister, Choura, both were advised to

go south on account of their health and there they fell in love with each other. One night, when Gertrude and I were taking a walk on the boulevard Saint-Michel, we met Choura in a short-sleeved open-at-the-neck dress and I said to her, Choura, you ought to cover yourself, that is not good for your health. She shrugged her shoulders and said, What does it matter? She was a beautiful, reckless creature.

René Crevel one day said that a friend of his, a professor at the University of Clermont-Ferrand, was an admirer of Sherwood Anderson's work and would be very pleased to meet Gertrude. I took it for granted that he was old man. But not at all, Monsieur Bernard Faÿ was a young man and went down once a week for three days to Clermont-Ferrand where he lectured. On the long train trips to and fro he worked not only at writing but typing. Virgil Thomson one day took us to meet him, and that was the beginning of our long friendship with Bernard Faÿ.

Virgil Thomson had become a Parisian through the influence of Bernard, who had him and the chorus from Harvard come to France to give concerts. I do not know whether Virgil went back to America again and returned to France or whether he stayed over in Paris. The first I remember was his invitation to spend an evening with him in his little room at Montmartre, where he played and sang the *Socrate* of Erik Satie. Virgil had a gift of producing an opera with only himself and a piano.

Later he had a studio on the Quai Voltaire with a small window from which you could see a small piece of the Seine below you. He had as an intimate friend a quite old lady, the widow of a professor, Madame Langlois, who had a caustic wit and was a good friend to Virgil. She was perhaps a little jealous of Gertrude's influence. She had taught Virgil everything about the French and France. One evening he gave a party. Madame Langlois took me by the arm and said, Come quickly, and I saw that she was leading me to André Gide whom I did not wish to have to greet in that way. He said to us, How do you do? Madame Langlois shaking one finger at him said, You have been very naughty not to come to see me. You will come, will you not? And he said, shaking one finger in front of her face, *Peut-être.*

When Madame Langlois died, it was discovered that she was thirteen years older than anyone knew. She was eighty-three years old.

Later Virgil had Maurice Grosser share the studio with him. At that time Maurice was a poor painter but a charming person – intelligent, witty and sensitive. They were both excellent cooks and prepared simple and delicious dinners.

When we first met Georges Maratier he was young, handsome and a soldier in a horizon blue uniform, the blue uniform of the First World War. Shortly after the war he was in his father's business, his father was a wholesale wine merchant and they had wonderful wine. Georges' father when he was pleased with his son would say, Come down, we will get some wine. They would go down into the wine cellar with a special basket for wine bottles and select some wine for Georges, because Georges had a flat for himself. Georges would bring us a few bottles of this wonderful wine which was not on the market.

Georges had met at Tchelitchev's house a young man named Bravig Imbs, an American. Bravig Imbs had come over from Dartmouth College where he had written a novel that had disturbed the wife of one of the professors, a character in the novel. He somewhat hastily left Dartmouth and came over to

Paris, where he met Tchelitchev and René Crevel and Georges Maratier. They found him astonishingly innocent.

Bravig wanted to be a writer and worked as a proofreader on two American newspapers in Paris. After he was thrown out of one he would go to the other, back and forth. Georges took a fancy to the poor young man and would take him in when Bravig had no money, give him a room in his flat and very good food. Bravig, even when he was desperately hard up, having lost one or both of his jobs, was always a little extravagant. He would, to Georges' horror, go to the smartest *coiffeur* in Paris to have his hair cut.

One night Bravig came into Georges' flat. He sat down in an armchair, and in his careless way he dropped his hat on one side and his stick on the other. Georges said, Do not do that, it does not suit my room to be careless like that, pick up your things. Well, said Bravig, I have had an experience. Whom do you think I met just now? Georges said, How do I know? Whom did you meet? Well, I met James Joyce, said Bravig. *Je ne connais pas ce Monsieur,* said Georges. Pick up your stick and behave yourself.

The next night Bravig came in throwing his stick on one side of the room and his hat on the other. Whom do you think I met today? he said to Georges. And Georges said, I'm sure I don't know. Gertrude Stein! said Bravig. I don't know the lady, said Georges. Which was, of course, one of Georges' amusements, for he was seeing Gertrude Stein very often at that time.

One day Georges said to me, If you will drive me down in your car to Dampierre, where Bravig is staying at a station hotel, we will have a very good lunch there and bring Bravig back with us, for he is once more out of both jobs. We had a very good lunch indeed. After lunch Georges said, Bravig, you come back to Paris with us, you cannot stay on here without any money. We will see about getting you a job. You do not have to go to the smartest barber in Paris to have your beautiful hair cut, you will have to learn the common economies of a young man about town.

One day a few years later, Bravig was invited to visit Danzig where he met a young Polish girl, Valeska, and he wrote to us he thought of bringing her back to Paris with him when he returned. Gertrude wrote him a sharp letter saying, You can't do that, Bravig, you can't bring a girl to whom you are not married back to Paris. And Bravig said, What do you propose I should do? Marry her, said she, which Bravig proceeded to do.

After Bravig returned to Paris, he and Valeska came to visit us rather often. When Valeska was pregnant they asked me to be the godmother of their child. I said, Oh no, Bravig, not that, you know what happened when I became the godmother of Hemingway's child, we didn't see him for the longest time.

It was Bravig Imbs who introduced to us Elliot Paul, who with Eugene Jolas had founded *transition*. Elliot Paul was a sincere admirer of Gertrude's work and understood it. She was asked by him to contribute "An Elucidation." At the same time that they were publishing Gertrude, they published James Joyce. *Ulysses* had already been published by Sylvia Beach and had met with a sensational success. Sylvia Beach had a little lending library and bookshop, Shakespeare and Company, to which Gertrude had been a subscriber. All of which Sylvia Beach has written about so entertainingly in her book, *Shakespeare and Company*.

Djuna Barnes had asked Gertrude if she and Mina Loy might bring James Joyce for tea one afternoon. To which Gertrude as usual said, Yes of course. But the afternoon they came,

they came without Joyce and made no excuse for his absence.
Evidently the idea of meeting Gertrude was not to his liking.
And it was only many years later when Gertrude went to tea
at Jo Davidson's that Sylvia Beach came across to her and
said, Would you mind coming over and meeting James Joyce?
and Gertrude said, Of course not. They said how do you do to
each other and James Joyce said, It is strange is it not that we
have never met, we are both writers and live in the same
neighborhood. Yes, said Gertrude. And that is all they had to
say to each other, they could not think of anything more to
say.

When Gertrude came back from the tea she wanted to tell
me about this episode. But I said, No, tell me about Lady
Mortimer Davis from San Francisco, I want to know what you
thought of her beauty. Gertrude had nothing to say about her.

Georges Hugnet had by this time become a publisher, he
had taken over the *Editions de la Montagne* from Georges
Maratier. Hugnet was devoted to Gertrude and translated, so
he felt, some of Gertrude's portraits.

Hugnet's big black eyes were like a mechanical toy, they
wandered about his white face in the manner of the man in the
moon. His father was an impossible little man who flirted with
young girls.

Georges' mother, a charming person and pretty, adored her
son. She once gave a dinner party for his friends, and Gertrude
and I were asked. Max Jacob was amongst the other guests and
he danced barefooted a dance that scandalized Madame Hugnet and did not amuse us very much.

Gertrude had not liked Max Jacob in those days. He was un-
tidy and possibly dirty. Gertrude did not like his humor.

One summer before the First World War he was with Pi-

casso in the country. Fernande asked me if I would like my
fortune told and I answered yes. She said, Max Jacob will
read your horoscope. Oh that is different, I said, that is not
telling fortunes. But he wrote it and Fernande said I could
give her some money which she would give to Max. The horoscope ended with what startled me, A tendency to theft. Years
later, when Max became a devout Catholic, he tried to get the
horoscope back from me because it was not Catholic. But it
was already at Yale.

Madame Hugnet had a few gems which she liked to wear
and one day Georges said, My mother is in deep trouble, the
fortuneteller says that she will lose something precious. But it
really was worse than gems. She lost her husband's affection.

It was at Georges Hugnet's that we saw a painting by a hand
which interested Gertrude. It was by Sir Francis Rose. Georges
spoke slightingly of Francis. One did not blame him, Francis
was a very difficult guest.

Gertrude became so deeply interested in the paintings of
Francis Rose that she bought all that she could find at his
picture dealer's. She told Georges Maratier that he should
locate and buy for her any pictures of Francis' that he could
find, and he gathered several. She hung them in the studio at
the rue de Fleurus.

Not long after this she met Meraud Guevara on the street
and Meraud said, Oh I was wondering if you were in town
because I wanted you to come this afternoon, there is going to
be someone at the house that you will want to meet. Francis
Rose.

Francis was there with his friend Carley Mills, and in their
pockets in turn was a Chihuahua dog named Squeak, after his
manner of talking. Francis got up and came and sat next to

Gertrude and she told him about the pictures she had of his and said that after tea was over they could go to the rue de Fleurus and see them. Which they did. Francis flushed rosy with the pleasure of seeing his pictures on the walls next to Picasso's.

Francis Rose was one of the many painters in whom Gertrude was interested after the First War. Another was Picabia, whom Gertrude Stein had met through Mabel Dodge years before.

Picabia was an only child. His father was a Spaniard from Seville and his mother was a Mademoiselle Charcot of the family of discoverers and scientists. His uncle, the brother of his mother, was curator of the library of Sainte-Geneviève.

Picabia had a distinct gift for painting and as a very young man left home surreptitiously for Switzerland and for freedom. When he came back to France he settled down to be a serious painter. Georges Maratier, when Gertrude became interested in Picabia's pictures, gave her a charming little landscape that Picabia had painted at about that time. He had become one of the earliest of the dadaists while he was in Switzerland.

His painting was uneven but indicative of the volatile character shown throughout his career. At moments there was a certain elegance in his work, at other times a certain brutality.

Kristians Tonny was a Dutch painter who had been in the 1926 show of the painters Tchelitchev, Christian Bérard and the two Berman brothers. Tonny's father had given up his own painting to have money to send his son to study painting in Paris.

Gertrude did not notice his painting at that time, but later when he was slightly under the influence of the surréalistes she bought several of his pictures in which Elliot Paul also was interested. Tonny painted a portrait of Gertrude and Basket which I gave to an American soldier.

Tonny had been an infant prodigy and a great many people had discovered him, one after the other, and had become his patrons.

Juan Gris was at this time a favorite of Gertrude. We had seen a good deal of the Gris' in Paris after they left the rue Ravignan and were living near their close friend Kahnweiler, the art dealer, at Auteuil. Gertrude gradually collected more of Juan's pictures and became devoted to him.

Juan in spite of his lack of health was a very gay, delightful companion. He and Josette rented a small house directly on the sea at Bandol and we went down and stayed at the inn there, spending our days with them. Juan took us on a walk over the rocks of the coast to see the country and Josette prepared plain but delicious food.

They knew at Bandol a bourgeoise family who had inherited from many past generations some very fine Flemish pictures and who were interested in the Gris'. They became intimate friends. Juan made portrait drawings of two of the young men and two other members of the family, Jeanne la Blonde and Jeanne la Brune. Juan was having such a desperate flirtation with Jeanne la Blonde that Josette was planning to separate from him. It was a desperate situation for her, but it ended all right. Soon, however, poor Juan died.

Juan had always had financial troubles, unlike Matisse. The Matisses, when they moved before the First War to a villa with a garden in which there was a statue of Paul and Virginie under an umbrella, had asked us out to lunch. The first thing Gertrude noticed when we came into the salon was a small but very fine Cézanne and she said, Matisse, you have a lovely picture there. And he said, Yes, I was tempted to buy it and I am not doing any injustice to my children for the money that it cost will be more than returned in its increased value. Afterward when we got into our taxi to go back to Paris I said to Gertrude, You see, that is the way Matisse saves his money. What does Pablo do? He keeps his own pictures as an inheritance.

When Gertrude could not again find a publisher she sold the beautiful Picasso painting of the girl with a fan held in the air, which quite broke my heart. And when she told Picasso, it made me cry. But it made it possible to publish the Plain Edition.

Gertrude had been published earlier by Robert McAlmon, the editor of the Contact Editions. McAlmon had published *The Making of Americans* but Gertrude and he did not remain friends. It was of McAlmon that Hemingway once said, I do not like to see him throw up my royalties.

McAlmon had at one time been married to Bryher, who had long been Hilda Doolittle's close friend. One day we took Thornton Wilder over to Bryher's house because he was an enthusiastic admirer of H.D. After we came away Thornton said, Bryher is Napoleonic, she walks like him, she talks like him, she probably feels like him.

Our first Plain Edition volume, *Lucy Church Amiably,* was badly printed in Paris. It would not stay closed and its back broke. So for a second volume, *How to Write,* we went down to Dijon. Gertrude wanted it to look like an eighteenth-century copy of Sterne which she had found once in London, bound in blue and white paper on board. But this was not very successful and I complained bitterly saying, Look how badly the pages fit each other. The printer said to me, What can you expect, madame? It is machine made, it is not done by hand. Which remained a classic answer for Gertrude and me.

Then one evening at a party we met Darantière himself – he had printed *The Making of Americans* – and I said to him, You must get me out of a mess, I have two books to print for Gertrude and I need you to help me. I want them to be inexpensive so that they can be sold in the United States for two dollars and a half and leave me with the postage and duty and a possible profit. Yes, he said, we shall do them in monotype, which is commercially cheap. I will come to see you and show you what I mean. Do not worry, it will come out all right. Was I always being told not to worry?

Darantière had a charming idea. He proposed to place each book in a cardboard slip cover of the yellow of the cover of *The Making of Americans.* One of the books was *Operas and Plays,* the other was *Matisse Picasso and Gertrude Stein.* There was still one left for me to do, *Before the Flowers of Friendship Faded Friendship Faded.* I bought some handmade peach-leaf paper and printed one hundred copies. The title came to Gertrude in the dining room of a hotel at Bourg when two guests of the hotel at two different tables were disagreeing.

In the summer of 1931 Aaron Copland and Paul Bowles came to visit us at Bilignin. We called Paul Freddy, I do not know why. The first time he came to dinner Bernard Faÿ was there. Bernard was very pleased with the young boy, for when Bernard said to him, What does your father do? he answered, without any embarrassment or hesitation, My father is a dentist.

One day, walking in Belley, Freddy stooped and picked up a handful of money and I said to him, Oh, do you often do that? Quite frequently, said Freddy.

Freddy, who at that time was composing music, told Gertrude that Aaron Copland had once said to him, If you do not work now when you are twenty, nobody will love you when you are thirty.

As we were going to Bilignin just before the last war, Freddy telephoned the morning of our departure. Can I bring my wife to see you? he said. We did not know he had married and there was no time, we were leaving. Gertrude never met Jane Bowles. I met her later in Paris after Gertrude died.

One day Madame de Clermont-Tonnerre came to see Gertrude and took off her hat and said, What do you think of it? She had had her beautiful hair cut. Gertrude said, It suits your head. That is what you will have to come to, said Madame de Clermont-Tonnerre.

That night Gertrude said to me, Cut off my braids. Which I agreed to do. The following day I spent gradually cutting it off, because I did not know how you did it, and I got it shorter and shorter. The more I cut off, the better Gertrude liked it. Finally, toward the end of the afternoon, it was done and the doorbell rang. Gertrude said, Oh do not go to the door. I said, Oh yes I will, I will see who it is. It was Sherwood Anderson and he said, giving Gertrude one look, You look like a monk.

Later Gertrude forgot that she had ever had two long braids.

In 1934 it was suggested by a lecture bureau that Gertrude should go to New York. While she was writing her lectures for America, Bernard Faÿ came to stay with us at Bilignin. He had wired, May I bring a young man with me? And Gertrude as usual said, Of course. He brought with him James Laughlin, the child of an enormously wealthy family in Pittsburgh.

That same evening our friends the d'Aiguys were at the house for dinner, and James Laughlin burst into the conversation on the subject of war. Bob d'Aiguy said to him, Hush, young man, you do not know anything about war. Our family has suffered in many ways from wars, so please hush until you know more about what you are talking about. Whereupon James Laughlin excused himself and went up to his room and had no dinner.

I now commenced to prepare the costumes for Gertrude's voyage – one to lecture in in the afternoon, one to lecture in on evenings, one to travel in, an odd dress or two. Gertrude also had her leopard-skin cap from which she refused to be parted. Having gathered the lectures and the clothes and our plans together, we went back to Paris where Bernard Faÿ got us passage on the S.S. *Champlain* at a reduced rate. I bought for Gertrude an endless quantity of lovely gloves and we were very nearly ready to leave.

At the boat train Trac, our Indochinese cook, Georges Maratier and James Laughlin were there to see us off when suddenly Gertrude said to me, There is a button off my shoe. How can there be? I said. There is, she said. Trac disappeared, found a needle and some linen thread and sewed the button on again. In this prosaic manner we went off on our great adventure.

9

GERTRUDE said that the boat trip had been very much improved. She did not know how little the trains had until we got to America. Going aboard the boat, there was a covered gangway so that though it was pouring no rain fell upon us. One does not go onto planes as protected as that.

On the boat I found lovely flowers from Madame de Clermont-Tonnerre. She had sent them to me because I had suggested her translating one of Gertrude's lectures.

The service on board the boat was extraordinary and the first

thing we discovered was that we could have taken one or both
of the dogs with us, so far as the boat was concerned; the difficulty would have been in hotels and on planes. The steward
came and said to me, They tell me madame that you have dogs
in Paris, why did you not bring them?

The steward asked us if we wished to have a table for ourselves in the dining room or if we wished to eat at the captain's
table. They seemed to think that Gertrude deserved that distinction, but we decided we preferred being alone. The *Champlain* had the best cooking imaginable and thereafter we ordered our meals in advance, cutting out endless courses.

After lunch we went up on deck, which was covered in glass
like a conservatory, where we were immediately spoken to by
a very pleasant doctor and his wife and little son from New
Jersey. They made our trip very pleasant. They went over to
Europe each year as good New Yorkers do.

There was on the boat a woman who read horoscopes, and
she told Gertrude that the American trip would be of the
greatest interest to her. Also on board the boat was the widow
of a general who had been killed the year we were in Touraine.
Very discreetly Gertrude and I were silent about his accidental
death. The widow sat at the captain's table and carried an immense feather fan.

When the captain came to speak to Gertrude, he asked her
why she was not at his table and would she care to come. She
said she was living very quietly on the boat, very happily, very
comfortably. He then said, would we come and have a drink
with him. Gertrude said, that even less than dinner. But we
went and met some promiscuous passengers.

On board was the Abbé Dimnet, whom we used to see at the
home of Alice Ullman. It was with Eugene Paul Ullman at

lunch at the Café Voltaire one Friday that he had asked us what we would care to eat. When I said, Sole for me, everybody ordered fish. Finally the maitre d'hôtel asked the Abbé what he was going to have and he said, As for me I shall have beefsteak.

Finally we landed in the bay of New York, quickly recognizing the skyscrapers and gradually finding ourselves next to friends on the dock.

Gertrude had made up her mind about the reporters, that if she must she would see them. The Abbé I think was surprised at the number of reporters that came to interview Gertrude. Amongst them was W.G. Rogers who said to me, I am alarmed at the number of questions they will ask her. I said to him, Oh you do not need to be, it will not disturb her. They wanted to know if she had come to instruct America and she said, Never, no, I have come to see and hear as well as to talk.

In the meantime I had made out the customs papers so that they would be ready in time. When we got off the boat Carl Van Vechten, Bennett Cerf and a cousin of Gertrude from Baltimore were there to meet us. I went over to the customs official and said, Here are the keys, there is nothing dutiable, I have declared the duty, the clothes that are new were made to be worn here by us, I do not think anything is dutiable. And I went back to talk to Carl. I looked over to see what the customs inspector was doing and found that he was doing nothing so I said to Carl, I think he is finished, of course I shall tip him. Carl threw up his hands in horror and said, Of course not. Well, I said, can I shake hands with him and thank him? Not shake hands, said Carl, you will not be doing that here.

The next week in *The New Yorker* there was a drawing supposed to represent the customs inspector saying, Gertrude says four hats is a hat is a hat.

Carl and Bennett came back for lunch to the Algonquin Hotel, where I had written for rooms. There was a dreadful commotion. The reporters had come back to the rooms, there were wires, there were coils, there were all sorts of impedimenta. I could not open my bag, I could not open my trunk, I could do nothing.

During the afternoon we got rid of the disturbances and went out for a walk. I proposed finding some fruit. To my surprise the attendant in a good fruit shop said to me, Miss Toklas, are you liking New York? How did he know who I was?

At Times Square I saw an electric light revolving. It said, Gertrude Stein has arrived in New York, Gertrude Stein has arrived in New York. As if we did not know it.

By the time we got back to the hotel lovely flowers and fruit from the Van Vechtens had arrived, and I commenced to put some order in our affairs and enjoy the fruit.

We had three rooms – two bedrooms and a sitting room – and we were to have these for our stay.

It was getting dark and we decided to have supper in our rooms. Gertrude thought that she would get the habit at once of eating very lightly in the evening so that she could lecture when it was necessary without changing her diet. She thought that oysters and honeydew melon would be a satisfactory diet.

Mr. Harcourt, who had published *The Autobiography of Alice B. Toklas* by Gertrude Stein, had sent us word that if we could come to see him the next morning he would like to show us their editorial rooms and have us meet Mr. Brace. So the next morning we went over there.

Mr. Harcourt said, I had no idea you were going to be as

popular as this. Gertrude said, No, but you should have thought so because it is the things they do not understand that attract them the most. Mr. Harcourt thereupon sent for Mr. Brace and said, Listen to what she says, she says the public is attracted to what it does not understand.

There was a slight contretemps with the lectures at Columbia University. There were three lectures to be given there and they now sent word to Gertrude that fifteen hundred people was all the hall could hold, what were they to do with the audience. Gertrude had me write that it had been understood definitely that not more than five hundred would be present at any lecture, what did they mean. And over came the head of the lecture service saying what did *we* mean. I asked him if he had not received word from Paris about the number of people to be admitted to each lecture. Oh, he said, I did not think you meant it. Why did you suppose, I said, that it was said and not meant? Gertrude said, It is simple, if you cannot agree to that dismiss the idea of the lectures. We cannot do that, he said. Well, said Gertrude, I give you twenty-four hours – that is, until tomorrow morning – to let me know. They came to see her point of view very pleasantly.

At the lecture at Columbia University I found Gertrude's old friend Mabel Weeks sitting next to me and she said very possessively, Am I not going to see Gertrude? To which I was forced to answer, I am sorry but I do not know. Miss Weeks was one of her old friends whom she was not intending to see. Another was Mrs. Mills, Carley Mills's mother, who rang me up to see if we would dine with her at her home. I said that I regretted it was not going to be possible, that Gertrude was not accepting invitations.

We went to Princeton University one evening for a lecture.

The lecture room was filled, but not with more than five hundred people. The train service was very poor. The train was late in arriving at Princeton and much later still in arriving in New York, so that it was a fatiguing journey.

Carl was giving us parties to meet his Negro friends, who somewhat scandalized me by their outspokenness. A very distinct memory was the blue-eyed blond Negro who had chosen to remain black, Mr. Walter White, whom later I was to know as the husband of a friend, Poppy Cannon. There was also present at this party James Weldon Johnson.

At another party there were Mr. and Mrs. Knopf. Mrs. Knopf had come to Gertrude in Paris, probably through Mrs. Bradley the literary agent. Mrs. Knopf wanted a manuscript of Gertrude Stein to publish, so Gertrude had said she would find one for her and sent it to her before she left Paris. Months after, there had been no word from Mrs. Knopf so Gertrude said to me, Write to her and ask her for the return of the manuscript, she has kept it long enough. Whereupon Mrs. Knopf wrote to Gertrude saying that Gertrude knew how much she wanted the manuscript for their firm but that when she got home the boys in the office said it would not do.

There were innumerable lunches and dinners. On one occasion Carl introduced George Gershwin to Gertrude Stein, and he played some of his music for her.

Carl took hundreds of photographs of Gertrude and quite a few of me in a very small hot room under glaring electric lights, which exhausted Gertrude. She was relieved when she was allowed to leave it. Carl took some perfect photographs of Gertrude with her many waistcoats as a background.

In the autumn of 1934 we went from New York to Chicago, to settle a misunderstanding as to what and where Gertrude

Stein was to lecture. Bobsy Goodspeed, whom we had seen in France, received us in her home and had us meet the people who were in charge of the lectures, particularly Fanny Butcher, who said there would be no difficulty and that she would undertake to make the schedule clear, which she promptly did.

It was to be in Chicago that Gertrude and I would see for the first time *Four Saints in Three Acts* performed. We were enchanted. It was not only that her opera was being performed that pleased her, but that Virgil Thomson's music and the stage settings were so beautiful.

Bobsy Goodspeed was interested not only in painting – she had a small Picasso and a number of other pictures – but in music and in the Russian ballet, an interest her husband did not share, so that one evening when a party was lasting quite late he suddenly appeared in his pajamas and said, It's time for you all to go home. But Gertrude Stein was particularly interested in Mr. Goodspeed, who was a Regent of the University and a leader of the Republican Party.

Gertrude Stein gave a lecture at the Arts Club of Chicago, of which Mrs. Goodspeed was the President. A great many people we knew or knew of were present. Their questions concerning painting interested them more than they did Gertrude.

Then Mrs. Goodspeed gave a tea party for Gertrude Stein to meet a great number of her friends. Amongst them was Hadley Hemingway Mowrer, Hemingway's first wife. It was her son to whom Gertrude and I were godmothers.

Gertrude also lectured at the University of Chicago. Mr. Robert Hutchins, President of the University, was personally a very charming person but very certain of what he wanted from Miss Stein. When he asked Miss Stein if she would undertake a meeting of the students under the direction of himself and

Mr. Mortimer Adler, she said, Why not? Well, he said, they aren't easy to manage. They have ideas of their own, but we will see.

So one evening they selected a group of students of their choice for the meeting and she said, Since we are here to discuss the things that interest you, you will ask me the questions. I would propose that we undertake to discuss what an epic is. Ah that, said one of them. Yes, she said, you must have ideas about this, and in getting down to your facts you will hear mine.

The discussion was fairly lively, and Gertrude Stein told me afterwards that she had the impression that both Mr. Hutchins and Mr. Adler thought she had allowed the students too much freedom. Both of them suggested that she should tell them what to think, to form their thoughts for them, and she replied, I have always allowed the young people to formulate their own ideas.

When the discussion was over, Mr. Adler said to Gertrude Stein, We are walking back to the home of the Hutchins' for dinner. As the four of us walked to the home of the President of the University, from where the meeting had taken place, Mr. Adler said, I never saw students so ready to talk as you made them. Oh, they always talk, said Gertrude Stein, they like to talk. Not for us, said Mr. Adler.

Mrs. Hutchins was a very charming, very pretty woman whose home was characteristically comfortable and elegant. At dinner, there was a sudden break when the maid came in and said to Mrs. Hutchins, but aloud, The police, madam. Mr. Adler drew back his chair, very red in the face, and said to Miss Stein, The police! And she said, Oh, that's quite all right, Miss Butcher is calling for us to go in the police car this evening.

Miss Butcher appeared, and we said good night to the Hutchins and went about to various places where the police were expecting trouble. A criminal was being followed and was expected to be caught that evening and we were to take part in this. When we had seen various parts of doubtful respectability, the police – there were two in the little car – said to Miss Stein, Where do you want us to take you? Where are you staying in Chicago? She gave them the address of the Goodspeeds, which was in an entirely different direction naturally. When we got there, Mrs. Goodspeed was entertained by the story of our adventure.

When Mr. Hutchins again came to see Gertrude Stein, he proposed that she undertake a series of lectures to some students in English whom Thornton Wilder had selected. Amongst them were two or three in whom Gertrude Stein became deeply interested and who remained in correspondence with her afterwards. The lectures were fairly lively but when Thornton Wilder proposed curbing some of the young men, she wafted him away.

At this time we returned to the East, and then went to Baltimore to visit Gertrude's cousin. In Baltimore we saw Fitzgerald again. It was the afternoon of Christmas Eve and he was expecting Zelda to return from the nursing home. She was permitted home for the holidays. When she arrived, their little daughter Scotty was brought down to the drawing room to greet her.

Gertrude Stein said, I have no Christmas gift for you, Scotty, I'm sorry, I did not know I was to see you. And Scotty said, Haven't you something in your pocket? Gertrude pulled out of her pocket a pencil, as I remember, and Scotty said, I shall keep this as a souvenir.

Zelda, who looked lovelier than ever, brought out some paintings she had lately done, and asked Gertrude to observe them. When Gertrude said she liked them, Zelda asked her to choose one for herself, which Gertrude did.

We also visited Washington and were taken to the White House, where we were received by Mrs. Roosevelt. The President was indisposed, she announced, and would be unable to meet us, to which Gertrude blandly said, Yes. Mrs. Roosevelt then informed us that one of the officials would receive us in his stead, to which Gertrude again said, Yes. He was a well-known official, but I have no recollection of who he was.

We returned to New York and went on to New England, where the Rogers' took us around in the car of their friend Mrs. Wesson, of the family of the manufacturer of the revolver. It was winter, and the New England churches in their white coats were like postcards.

We were driven to Vassar, where all the young ladies were beautiful and very smartly dressed. But Gertrude had to ask for a soft-boiled egg and an orange because she could not eat the food.

Now we went South. With Carl Van Vechten we went to Richmond, where we were introduced to Ellen Glasgow. At dinner I sat next to James Branch Cabell who asked me, Is Gertrude Stein serious? Desperately, I replied. That puts a different light on it, he said. For you, I said, not for me.

In Charleston, the camellia trees were very tall and full of red, pink and white flowers. There we had a very kind guide, a professor, who took us to see the oak trees which belonged to the Club of Centenarian Oaks. Gertrude Stein's lecture at Charleston was in a beautiful historic house, not very large, which interested me more than it interested Gertrude Stein.

She was delighted, however, by a sign near the airport of Atlanta, Buy Your Meat and Wheat in Georgia.

We flew to New Orleans and the plane hovered over the delta of the Mississippi and the sea in a quite frightening way. In New Orleans we met Sherwood Anderson, whom Gertrude Stein was delighted to see again. Sherwood took us about to show us the old quarter of New Orleans and the market and the homes of several of the old families, one of whom had a lovely Spanish name. He brought us some wonderful oranges, very sweet and very juicy, not at all like the oranges we had had in France, and he peeled them for us, saying, You can eat them now, which was very Western of him. He showed us where they gathered the wild rice we had eaten at Thanksgiving in New England. The gathering was a risky procedure.

From New Orleans we flew to Fort Worth and then to Chicago, where we stayed at Thornton Wilder's apartment. Eventually we went to Dallas, where we were to stay at Miss Ela Hockaday's school and where Gertrude Stein was to lecture. The flowers at Dallas, wild and cultivated, were wondrously beautiful, bright and fragrant, and the young pupils at the school were gay, interested and intelligent. Miss Stein spent her mornings wandering around with the girls and talking to them. At her lecture they showed astonishing understanding of her work. She also lectured at the Women's Club in Dallas, where a fairly lively discussion took place.

From Dallas we flew west on our way to California. In those days the plane came down in Arizona; then we rose again and flew most perilously between two mountains, descending suddenly in Los Angeles. There we had a letter from one of Carl Van Vechten's friends, whom we had met in New York. She asked me would Gertrude Stein dine with her and meet some of her friends, Charlie Chaplin amongst others. I am sure she would, I said, but don't have too many people at table. Eight? she asked. And I said, That would be perfect. Is there anybody she wants to meet who lives here? Yes, I said, she wants very much to meet Dashiell Hammett. I don't know him, she said, but I will try to get him.

The night of the dinner party she asked us to come at a quarter of eight. She said, Dashiell Hammett's editor would not give his address, but I found through the film director of his novel where he was and I wrote to him saying, 'Gertrude Stein is dining with me tomorrow evening, would you come and meet her?' and he wrote back and said, 'If you would permit me to bring the hostess I was to have had. Lillian Hellman.' To which our hostess had answered that that would be very nice. When we got there and Dashiell Hammett appeared, he said to Gertrude Stein, It's the first of April and when I received the invitation I said, 'It's an April Fool's joke.' Well, said Gertrude Stein, you see it isn't!

When Mr. Chaplin arrived I said to him, The only films we have seen are yours, which flattered him but which was not exactly exact.

Conversation at dinner was fairly lively. Mr. Chaplin had brought with him Paulette Goddard, who was an enfant terrible. There was also a Spanish diplomat and our hostess' brother, who was a film director. After dinner there were some guests who came, amongst them Anita Loos, to whom I took an immediate fancy. The film directors gathered around Miss Stein and said, We would like to know how you came to have your enormous popularity, and she said, By having a small audience, whereupon they shoved their chairs away from her, discouraged with what she had to advise.

Gertrude Stein rented a drive-yourself car and we went north by way of Santa Barbara and the coast to Monterey, which to my astonishment had become a prosperous, busy little town instead of the charming village it was when I used to stay there as a young girl. There were traffic regulations which we had evidently ignored, for a policeman came up and said, What are you doing here, ladies? and I answered, I am trying to find Madame Bonifacio's adobe home, where I used to stay. He said, They have moved it up into the hills. Moved an adobe house? I said. Oh, yes, he said, Eastern millionaires do that. And Sherman's rosebush? I said. Did that go up into the hills with the house?

We got to the Del Monte Hotel quite late that night and at once there was a telephone call from Mabel Dodge. I answered. She said, Hello, when am I going to see Gertrude? and I answered, I don't think you are going to. What? said she. No, said I, she's going to rest. Robinson Jeffers wants to meet her, she said. Well, I said, he will have to do without.

The food at the Del Monte was as marvelous as I remembered it from my youth and they had on their menu abalone, a dish that until then was unknown to me. We rested there for several days, and then went to San Francisco on the day that the first airplane started for Honolulu.

In San Francisco, traffic on the hills was well arranged but seemed to us to be fairly dangerous. However, Gertrude Stein slipped into a vacant spot around the corner from the hotel. We got settled in rooms overlooking the Golden Gate, filled with flowers from Carl Van Vechten's friend, Gertrude Atherton, and my friend, Clare de Gruchy, and from the ladies of the American Women's Club.

Coming back to my native town was exciting and disturbing.

It was all so different, and still quite like it had been. Shortly there was a telephone message from two old friends, Hilda and Faufie Brown, who wanted to know if there was anything they could do for me. The Women's Club of San Francisco sent two of their members to arrange for the lecture. On the way to it on the following day, Gertrude Stein was taken in charge by these ladies and I met in the hallway Sidney Joseph, another old friend, the brother of Nellie Jacot. Not possible, I said. I didn't expect to see you. Well, here I am, he answered.

I went in to the lecture hall alone, seeing an endless number of familiar faces who bowed and waved their hands to me. I settled down as quietly as I could, but found that there were too many people who wanted to speak to me. My very dear friend, May Coleman, bowed and nodded as if it hadn't been almost thirty years since I had spoken to her last.

The discussion after the lecture was fairly commonplace, but the crowd of people who hovered around Gertrude Stein was more lively. It had been understood that Gertrude Stein would sign books, but there were a number of people who said to me, When that is over can we meet Gertrude Stein and drive you back to your hotel? One of them said to me, You know we were tremendously fond of your father, your mother was an angel, and you are very dear to us. I noted the descending order.

Gertrude Stein lectured next at the University of California. There we discovered that the desert flowers were at their height and that we could see them in the northern section by driving down to it, which we did on the following day. The rare specimens that we saw were indeed a wondrous display.

Gertrude Atherton had asked us to lunch with her at a special fish restaurant on the wharf and to a dinner in honor of Gertrude Stein to meet a number of people. Miss Stein was introduced to someone who asked her where she was born and when she answered, In Pittsburgh, Pennsylvania, he was shocked. It should have been California as I used to say, but there was no persuading her to change her place of birth.

We went to the site of my birth, for the Fire had consumed the house, and to the home where my father and I had lived before I came away. One of the bridges was being built, which would, it seemed to me, destroy the landscape a good deal.

Mrs. Atherton took us to the convent at San Rafael, where her granddaughter was a nun. Mrs. Atherton said the nun in charge was a San Franciscan and adored San Franciscan gossip, so that we would have to talk to her. The convent was beautifully situated amongst trees and flowers, and we had a charming afternoon there. From San Francisco we had planned to go north to Seattle but that was going to take too much time, so we arranged to take the plane to Omaha. Planes were slow in those days, and the stop at Omaha would be less fatiguing. The crossing over the Sierras gave us a landscape more beautiful than anything I have ever seen.

After Omaha we went to Chicago, where we stayed with Bobsy Goodspeed. There we saw again Thornton Wilder, who for so many years retained a place in our hearts.

This was the beginning of the end of our American visit, for we had not too much time to get back to Paris. Carl Van Vechten said to Gertrude, You will no longer be disturbed by strangers who want to speak to you. And Bernard Faÿ said to me, Does this persistence of the population in wanting to speak to Gertrude Stein not annoy her? No, I said, to her it is exactly like the country neighbors at Bilignin.

So from New York we sailed back to France on the same boat, the *Champlain,* that had brought us six months before.

On the boat a message came to us from Pavlik Tchelitchev asking Gertrude Stein to meet him and a friend who was on board, to which she graciously said Sure, though she did not want to see him. The boat was as comfortable and the food as exquisite as it had been when we came over.

In Paris we unpacked the books and the possessions we had gathered in the United States and got ready to go to Bilignin. We picked up our dogs, Basket and Pépé. Basket was in the Bois de Boulogne. When we went there he was not to be found because he had been taken for a walk, so we had to wait for him. But Pépé, who was staying with the Maratiers, jumped for joy into our arms as he originally did when he came to us.

Bilignin seemed quieter and lovelier than we remembered. We planted at once for the spring the vegetables and American corn, and got to work on our garden. I commenced to gather the *fraises des bois,* a never-ending task.

10

—

Summers in Bilignin were always very busy, enjoyable, and productive. Vegetables had become a passion, flowers always had been, my work in the garden was a pleasure. Occasionally it got me into trouble. One day I climbed on a case to reach the tallest of the French string beans growing on a rod. The case collapsed and I fell; down came the beans on top of me. Gertrude Stein considered me too adventuresome and said, Fewer vegetables would leave us still with enough variety.

Our neighbor, the Baroness Pierlot, had cultivated fifty-seven varieties, like the Heinz pickles, and I did not think I should have less. But the more I grew, the more I cooked, so that by the end of the day I wasn't fit for much else.

Madame Pierlot and Paul Claudel, the great poet, were old and dear friends. They met frequently, as he had bought a château not far from Béon.

Madame Pierlot had been born a Catholic, but – as Bernard Faÿ once said – she had been converted to Jean Jacques Rousseau and never had lost her new faith. One day she said to Gertrude, I have had enough of Claudel's lecturing me on my religion, he should leave me alone to go my own way. If he talks to me about it again I shall get up and go away. Gertrude said, You will not do that. No, she said, but I shall devise something.

She returned to the subject the next time she and Gertrude met. I have found means of stopping Claudel, she said. Oh? said Gertrude. Yes, she said, I told him outright I was perfectly happy without his converting me back to Mother Church and he said, 'Oh that's all right, I know that when I go to heaven I will find you with arms outstretched, waiting to welcome me.' 'Who told you I was to die first?' Madame Pierlot replied.

Before we left New York, Thornton Wilder had proposed that Gertrude and I remain there and he would find us a house in Washington Square. Gertrude was attracted to the idea, but it was never mentioned by her again. Now Thornton came to visit us at Bilignin.

I planted a common kind of orchid that Gertrude and I found at a Geneva horticulturist. The roots were fantastically surrealist, like an outstretched hand. When I put them into the ground and covered them, I did not expect to see anything grow. But a nice little orchid did grow, and it filled an empty spot in one of the twenty-six flower beds on the terrace.

I grew also a mallow that produced many kinds and colors of large flowers, which were very effective in vases for the house as well as in the garden. Gerald Berners took one of my pots of mallows, placed it on a table in the garden, and painted it. Pierre Balmain came over from Aix-les-Bains and undertook to make bouquets for me, but Gerald had more experience and made them with greater success.

We returned to Paris at the summer's end, and Gertrude prepared for her lectures at Cambridge and Oxford. We went there in January. As before, they were a marvelous success.

The following year we were again in England, for "A Wedding Bouquet" was to be produced. Gerald Berners had written the music for the ballet. We stayed at Faringdon House, his country estate, and Gerald played his music, which was charming and gay.

At Faringdon House there was every year a celebration when a white horse was received in the drawing room. The horse belonged to Mrs. John Betjeman. He had been trained to walk up the steps, to come into the drawing room and to kneel there, where he would be given his tea when we had ours. All this without disturbing in the least the many lovely flowers and objects in the room.

After a few days at Faringdon House, we went up to London for the rehearsals at Covent Garden. Ninette de Valois was in charge of the production and consulted with Gertrude Stein and Daisy Fellowes.

On the evening of the first performance there were a number of people in the audience whom Gertrude Stein knew. After the performance, she and Gerald Berners appeared to receive the applause and bow to the audience.

Somerset Maugham came up to me to inquire about the

people in Paris. He wanted to know what to expect socially for himself.

While we were in England we visited our good friends the Abdys. We had first met them when they lived in France, and had dined with them at their fabulous house in Saint-Germain. I remember that when we arrived I had looked about and, not doubting that it was all reconstructed, took its wonder very easily. But it was all real.

It was Bertie, Sir Robert Abdy, who had said to Gertrude, You should write the history of your friends and time. Which she did, *The Autobiography of Alice B. Toklas.* It was outside the beautiful garden of his home, as we were going off in the car, that the suggestion was made. Shortly after, the Abdys decided to leave Saint-Germain on account of the English tax on absent landlords and they bought the house in Cornwall where we now stayed.

When the Abdys left Saint-Germain, Lady Diana heard that at the Ritz Bar there was a man who undertook to smuggle dogs into England on a steam launch. She entrusted to him her little Pekinese. The little Pekinese had been taught several charming tricks. One was, Die for your king and country. He would lie down on the ground and pretend to be dead.

Bertie was a great gourmet. He spent an hour every evening with his cook, discussing the food that had been prepared that day and was to be prepared for the next. Once I asked him, when I was sitting next to him at lunch, Of what is this sauce made? He said, looking at me, The dairy and the barn yard, I suppose.

While we were staying with them Alec Waugh was also a guest, and Sir Kenneth and Lady Clark. He supposedly was interested in modern painters but shied clear from committing himself. In the best English manner after dinner they played guessing games, at which I was extremely bad.

One afternoon we visited Dartmoor to see the Druidic white horse. Lovely Lady Diana on her knees prayed to it. It was only afterward, when her prayer had been granted, that she told us her prayer had been for a child.

After returning to Paris we discovered we would have to move from the rue de Fleurus. The landlord was giving our pavillon as a residence to his son, who was marrying. We thought it would be difficult to leave, but it was not.

We found a new place at the rue Christine, a dull, dark, short little street, through Meraud Guevara, who lived in the rue Dauphine nearby. When we saw the little street we were dubious, but when we saw the apartment we were thrilled. Gertrude immediately said, Have you enough money to tip the concierge liberally? I said I had. But the concierge refused to accept it, saying it was for the landlord to determine whether we were acceptable tenants.

So we moved into the rue Christine, and continued to alternate between Paris and Bilignin.

One summer day, in 1939, we received a visit from Clare Boothe Luce and her husband. They had been to Poland and were convinced that there would be war. We lunched with them at Belley, and then they came over and spent the following day with us at Bilignin. She was embroidering in petit point a map of the United States. She was convinced her husband would become President.

Rumors of war were, of course, flying. One night, when Cecil Beaton was there and had gone out for a long walk in the dark, someone came and said war had been declared. Gertrude said, Don't bother me, Cecil is lost, I must find him first.

When war was declared, there was immediately a great flurry. Gertrude and I obtained passes permitting us to use the roads, and we drove hurriedly to Paris. At the rue Christine we commenced to take down the pictures to protect them from concussion from the bombs. But we found that there was less room on the floor than on the walls, so the idea was abandoned. Our passports were not to be found, but our poodle's pedigree was. Which was fortunate, as it enabled us to obtain a ration for Basket II during the Occupation.

We returned immediately to Bilignin. War was at our gate and the American Consul at Lyon soon telephoned us to say we should leave at once, while leaving was still possible. Gertrude at first paid no attention to this. Then, the following day, she said, It might be wise to have our passports renewed. We drove to Lyon, but the Consulate was so filled with people that we did not wait.

On the way back to Bilignin we ran into Dr. and Mrs. Chaboux. Gertrude asked, What are you doing here? and Mrs. Chaboux answered in a matter of fact way, We have come to have our permit to hunt renewed. Ah, said Gertrude Stein. Yes, said Dr. Chaboux, game will help us to live. Gertrude Stein told them why we had been to Lyon and he said, Oh, don't think of leaving, one is always better where one belongs than hunting a refuge.

So we stayed on, with the guns getting nearer and nearer. One day we went to Aix-les-Bains, where Gertrude in her customary voice bought some books. The Germans had been there from the time they conquered France. I said to Gertrude, Take care, don't speak English so loud. She said, Nothing counts any more. The man at the ticket office in the station, who overheard, said to me, Are you English? We said, No, we're Americans. Oh, he said, don't worry, they'll be leaving soon.

One day we ventured into Belley, to gather such food as we could find and tobacco for me. Suddenly a German armored car rolled down the main street. We climbed into our car and came back to Bilignin in great haste.

The day the German troops came into Belley to stay, the Gestapo in small numbers came as well. The Germans noticed us in our car with Basket, and Pépé whom they could not see, and said, What a beautiful dog, to which we paid no attention.

Gertrude Stein's car had been converted, so that it ran on wood alcohol instead of gasoline. One day we drove over to see the Baroness Pierlot. She was to introduce us to the black market. It is not a matter of money, she told us, it is a matter of personality. One buys on the black market with one's personality.

Food was of course restricted and there was not much fuel. One day Madame Pierlot went up to her attic, where she used to find for her little granddaughter clothes to dress up in, the way little girls like to do. This time it was to find clothes for them all. It was winter and very cold; at best the château was mildly heated. Madame Pierlot stayed up there too long. When she came down she had caught cold, and pneumonia developed. She lived only a very few days and died. She said to Gertrude while she was sick, When I hear my sons talking of the war and I am in my room, I do not know what war it is, whether it is this war or the war of '14–'18 or the war of '70. Madame Pierlot said the clouds had become Hitlerian and as long as they were, the war would go on.

Poor little Pépé had suffered so from the cold, he would not go outside any more to do his duties. Finally I said to Gertrude

Stein, We have to take him to the vet's at once. And I said to the vet when I got to Aix-les-Bains, You will do what you can for him but I fear that this will be impossible. He said, There is no saving him, I shall have to give him an injection. I kissed little Pépé and put him in the basket I brought him in, a very pretty Spanish one that Madame Chaboux had given me, and I shook the vet's hand and I said, I will see you later. I could not see where I was walking for the tears. We will sit down somewhere for a moment, said Gertrude, and then have lunch and go back to Bilignin.

The years of the Occupation passed slowly. One of our greatest challenges was the securing of food. At this time I dreamed once of a long silver dish, floating on air. On it were three large slices of ham. The dream haunted me for months.

We were ejected from our home in Bilignin. The French army had been dissolved, and the landlord had no other place to put his family. Through friends of Madame Pierlot we found a large, rather pretentious home on a hill near Culoz, farther up the Rhône.

We were warned now, as we had been before, to leave France, to leave for Switzerland. But we decided against it. We packed our belongings and moved to Culoz, never to return to Bilignin again.

At one point Germans, two officers and their orderlies, were billeted in the house. Rooms were hastily prepared for them, and provisions were hidden. When they left, after two weeks, we heaved a deep sigh of relief.

Then came some Italians. The war in our corner of the world was nearly over. When news reached the Italians that their country had surrendered, they tore up their military papers. Gertrude Stein said to their officers, You should not have allowed them to do this. They were a kind of protection and you are without any now. You are at the mercy of the Germans. And sure enough the poor Italians, when they were forced to leave, could not escape and the Germans killed them all.

One day we thought we heard someone singing the "Marseillaise," and that was the beginning of the end. But once again there were Germans in the neighborhood, and a great many of them were billeted with us. The servants and I prepared beds and rooms for them amidst hideous confusion. At last they left, though not before helping themselves to our small supplies. One thing they overlooked were my jars of candied fruits, which I had been saving for the Liberation.

As the American forces advanced, a voice on the radio told us that Paris was free. The young girls in the town who had been friendly towards the Germans were soon having their heads shaved. Amongst them was a young Polish girl who had worked for us for a while. A man who kept the little general shop began selling small French flags and Gertrude came back with a handful, one of which we pinned into Basket's woolly hair.

The remaining Germans now tried to flee. A young man who had worked in our garden came down with his companions from a hill, where they had been throwing rocks on the railroad tracks to prevent the German trains from moving. In a very short while they had pushed the Germans into a corner and, with the aid of the Résistance, had wiped them out.

We celebrated by going to Belley. There we saw our first American jeep. We were jubilant. When the soldiers accepted our offer of dinner and lodgings for the night, we returned triumphantly to Culoz.

Several days later, when some friends, including Madame

Chaboux, had joined us for lunch, Clothilde the cook came running up the stairs from the kitchen. Madame, she called out, there are Americans at the door! To which Gertrude Stein said, Show them in, Clothilde. Amongst them were Eric Sevareid and Frank Gervasi. Gertrude flew to the door to kiss them and Madame Chaboux said, Does she know them? I said, Oh no, they are Americans. Oh yes, said Madame Chaboux, shocked as a French woman would be.

Eric Sevareid, whom Gertrude had known in Paris, said, I have just seen Francis Rose in London and met his wife. His wife? said we. Ah yes, said Sevareid, he's married a very pretty young woman, and he says he flew over Bilignin and dropped roses on the house. That, I said, is a Francis invention. Probably, said Sevareid, but I have brought you a photograph of his wife. To be sure, she was a very pretty young woman.

Eric Sevareid asked Gertrude Stein if she would go down to Voiron and make a broadcast to America. If she would, he would call for her in his jeep. He called for us, in fact, in two jeeps.

Gervasi, at Voiron, offered to take back Gertrude Stein's manuscript to New York. He was flying back on an American airplane the following day, so that night I sat down and typed everything that Gertrude had been careful to hide during the German Occupation. It was published by Random House as *Wars I Have Seen.*

Our relief at the Germans having left France was almost enough consolation for all that had happened to France, though goodness knows France had suffered woefully and had changed. I commenced now to make the fruit cake that was to follow the Peace. We had met some officers in Aix-les-Bains who asked Gertrude Stein if they might come to see her. When she said, What are you? and they said, Colonels, she answered that she had met a good many colonels. Well, said one of them, if you let us come we can produce a general, General Patch. The General, however, was unable to come, although he wrote Gertrude Stein a very gracious letter saying that he hoped to visit us soon.

So I prepared for him a Liberation Fruit Cake, using the dried fruits and peels I had kept hidden since the time of the invasion. A colonel from General Patch came up for the cake when it was done.

Life after the Liberation was confused and uncertain. We wanted to get back to Paris as soon as we could, but between our possessions and events we were delayed. Finally, one night in December, I got our possessions into a truck we had hired. In a car we also had hired – Gertrude had given her car to the Red Cross – we set off with our bags and Basket for Paris. It was good-bye forever to Culoz. I have never had the heart to go back there.

The night was cold and rainy. Not knowing what roads were passable, we found our way with difficulty in the dark. It was an arduous journey.

When daylight was about to appear, we were stopped by two men and a woman. The woman was holding a gun. What do you want? Gertrude Stein asked, and they said, We are the Résistance and we have come to see who and what you are, and where you are going and what you are doing here. They leaned over on to a Picasso portrait and I said, Take care, that is a painting by Picasso, don't disturb it. And they said, We congratulate you, madame, you may go on.

We got into Paris by daylight. The city was in the utmost confusion. There were new one-way streets and endless colored lights, but the police were kind enough to tell us how and where to turn.

It was wonderful to get back to the rue Christine and to find everything still there, at least so I thought then. But the next morning there was a great deal of change to accept. When I got up to show our little maid where the kitchen materials were, I was shocked to discover that everything had been rifled. A little footstool of petit point that I had made after a design of Picasso, the Louis XV silver candlesticks, and a few other precious objects were gone. Only then did I realize that the Germans had tied some of the pictures, ready to take them away.

I found what I could in the kitchen to make some coffee, and then Picasso came in. He and Gertrude embraced, and all of us rejoiced that the treasures of our youth, the pictures, the drawings, were safe.

We had brought with us a large, very beautiful Henri IV table, which Picasso now admired. Do you want it? I said. He said, Yes. Well, I said, take it now, we have no place for it here.

11

WE settled down in Paris, and life became busier than it had ever been. We received a great many visitors and took what seemed like a great many trips. Gertrude Stein and I toured Germany for several days, which Gertrude wrote about for *Life*. It was in an American bomber that we went. We also went to Belgium, where Gertrude Stein spoke to the American soldiers stationed there.

We met Joseph Barry, who has remained such a good friend.

Joe was at that time with the American army that liberated Paris. He came to ask Miss Stein to lecture to some troops.

We had received a visit from Norman Holmes Pearson just after our return. He was serving with the O.S.S. and had been flown into France. He asked us if we wished to put in a claim for the items looted by the Germans, but we declined. When he came he brought with him Perdita, Hilda Doolittle's daughter. We had known her as a child, when she lived in Switzerland with H.D. and Bryher.

Our home again became a salon. There were almost constant visits from American G.I.'s. One day we had a call from seven of them, all of them claiming to be poets. One of them asked if he might read his poem, but Gertrude suggested that he leave the manuscript instead. On reading the poem later, Gertrude discovered that it was by John Donne. She was furious, of course, and the young man was never welcome again.

There was, however, a genuine poet, George John, who came to the door one day. He asked if he could see Miss Stein and dragged from his pocket a sheaf of poems, which fluttered to the floor. What do you want? I said. I want her to read them, he replied. I'll ask her to, I said. And she did, and was wildly impressed. Where is he? she asked, but he was not to appear for another week. When he came back, Henry Rago, an editor of *Poetry,* was there. Gertrude introduced them, and some of the young man's poems were published in *Poetry* magazine.

Richard Wright was another of the American writers who visited Gertrude Stein after the war. He had long been an admirer of "Melanctha," the second story in *Three Lives,* which he considered one of the most important influences on his own career. He had been troubled at home by the problem of prejudice. Gertrude encouraged him to live in Paris, which he did.

Gertrude Stein had by this time resumed work on *The Mother of Us All*. It was based on the life of Susan B. Anthony, and introduced a number of historic figures and a few fictitious ones as well. The opera, with music by Virgil Thomson, was not produced until after Gertrude's death.

When Pierre Balmain came to Paris to establish himself after the war, Gertrude and I went to his first showing. Pierre had made earlier a suit for Gertrude Stein, and a suit and coat for me. When we went to his collection I said to her, For God's sake, don't tell anybody that we're wearing Pierre's clothes. We look too much like gypsies. Why not? said Gertrude, they're perfectly good clothes.

Cecil Beaton had accompanied us to the showing and he and Gertrude both wrote about Pierre's clothes. That same year Pierre asked me to write an article about his winter collection, which he later published in book form. Pierre created clothes according to the form of the woman's body, so that arms became more important than they had been. He was influenced by pictures he liked, amongst them those of Renoir.

Suddenly, Gertrude Stein was no longer well, and the doctor who came to see her said she should see a specialist because he thought her illness might become grave. But Gertrude rejected the idea and went on as usual. She even bought herself a little car. One day, driving in it along the rue des Grands Augustins, we met at the door of his home Picasso. Is this the car you have bought? he said. She said, It's not the car you wanted me to buy, and he said, Oh dear no, and she said, I don't like second-hand cars and that's what you proposed. She then looked up at Picasso and said, Why are you so cross? He said, I'm *not* cross.

Oh yes you are, she said, and he said to me, What's the matter with Gertrude? Nothing, I said, she simply doesn't agree with you about the kind of car she should buy. Gertrude Stein said, It's what I wanted and I've gotten it. So good-bye Pablo. And he said rather sullenly, Good-bye, and they never saw each other again.

A few days later Joe Barry came and took us to see an old friend, Noël Murphy, at Orgeval. Noël sang for Gertrude, and Joe then drove us back to the rue Christine.

Bernard Faÿ had offered us the use of his county home, and several days later, with Joe Barry, we drove down to Luceau. Joe stayed with us for a day or two. He was to take the train back to Paris, but first he took us for a drive. On the road Gertrude Stein was taken ill and we stopped at Azay-le-Rideau, where we had once considered buying a home. The lovely house had been sold and the château no longer had its park of woods about it.

Gertrude's illness was frightening. At the inn at Azay they gave us a room and sent for a doctor who said, Your friend will have to be cared for by a specialist, and at once! So I called Allan Stein, Gertrude's nephew, and asked him to meet us at the train the next day. When we went to board the train, Gertrude Stein refused to have a nurse or anyone take care of her, but ran around from one side of the train to the other to look out on the landscape.

When we got to Paris we were shocked to find an ambulance waiting to drive her to the American Hospital. She was not prepared for this, but there was nothing she could do and she put up with it. At the hospital she thanked Allan, and went to bed quite comfortably.

The next morning a consultation of the doctors of the hospital and of friends of the Allan Steins took place. The doctors said she was seriously ill and there could be no operation for several days. During this time Gertrude Stein was quite cheerful and not in any pain.

Then, however, the surgeons refused to perform the operation, saying she was not in a fit condition any more. But amongst the surgeons was one who said, I have told Miss Stein that I would perform the operation and you don't give your word of honor to a woman of her character and not keep it. So I shall operate.

By this time Gertrude Stein was in a sad state of indecision and worry. I sat next to her and she said to me early in the afternoon, What is the answer? I was silent. In that case, she said, what is the question? Then the whole afternoon was troubled, confused and very uncertain, and later in the afternoon they took her away on a wheeled stretcher to the operating room and I never saw her again.

Index

177